BALANCING THE DEVELOPMENT AGENDA

THE TRANSFORMATION OF THE WORLD BANK UNDER JAMES D. WOLFENSOHN, 1995–2005

Ruth Kagia, editor

THE WORLD BANK
Washington, D.C.

1818 H Street, NW
Washington, DC 20433
Telephone 202-473-1000
Internet www.worldbank.org
E-mail feedback@worldbank.org

1 2 3 4 08 07 06 05

Library of Congress Cataloging-in-Publication Data has been applied for.

ISBN: 0-8213-6173-2
EAN: 978-0-8213-6173-21
e-ISBN: 0-8213-6175-0

In early 1995 I had to nominate a new President of the World Bank at a time when the institution faced unprecedented challenges. The Cold War was over, but the new world was even more divided between the rich and the poor. The World Bank was under pressure from stakeholders and external critics and was seeking a new approach that would be more effective than the structural adjustment policies of the past decade and more responsive to the needs of the transition economies of Eastern Europe. The new President had to meet the challenge of leading development assistance efforts in the post–Cold War era. Jim Wolfensohn embraced it creatively, vigorously, and effectively.

Looking back over the many discussions I have had with Jim, one constant has been his passion for unleashing the tremendous potential of the World Bank to serve the world's poorest people. As President of the World Bank he has challenged the notion of what *could* be done and focused his leadership on what *should* be done. This has led to a revolution in how the Bank does business. He has made poverty reduction the raison d'être of the Bank, put the client at the driver's seat, and focused the institution on results. Early on in his tenure, he offered as his measure of development success "the smile on a child's face." His attention to putting people first has moved the Bank towards a two-pronged strategy: investment in people and investment in growth. There is a lot to show for these efforts: the Bank has been central in the design and implementation of major debt relief; it is at the forefront in fighting corruption to ensure that development aid reaches the intended beneficiaries; and it has emerged as one of the largest funders of HIV/AIDS programs.

We have all come to understand that long lasting peace and security can only be built on successful development and empowerment, where all people have the opportunity to participate in and benefit from the global economy. Jim's mantra "a world out of balance" has become a rallying cry for change. This book outlines the various ways in which the World Bank has focused on actions to help redress this imbalance, for example: the intensified focus on Africa and other low income countries; programs to help close the digital divide such as WorldLinks; the African Virtual University; and the scaling up of programs to reduce social and economic inequality.

In our increasingly interdependent world the challenge of fighting poverty is greater than ever before. The achievements of the past ten years have demonstrated what can be done when the world joins together over a common issue, whether it is getting girls into school or rallying behind the victims of a devastating tsunami. Jim Wolfensohn's tenure has left the World Bank much better equipped to address the challenges of the 21st century. This book of reflections by some of the individuals who have worked most closely with Jim in shaping the new development agenda is at once a record of his accomplishments and a guidepost to the work we all still have before us. I hope it finds a wide readership.

In 1966 Robert Kennedy spoke these now immortal words in South Africa:

"Each time a man stands up for an ideal, or acts to improve the lot of others, or strikes out against injustice, he sends forth a tiny ripple of hope and crossing each other from a million different centers of energy and daring, those ripples build a current that can sweep down the mightiest walls of oppression and resistance."

Jim's dream of a world free of poverty sparked a ripple of hope which has, in ten short years, set in motion a current that is sweeping across the world offering hope to the world's poorest people.

William Jefferson Clinton
42nd President of the United States
May 2005

Boxes

THIS BOOK WAS PREPARED BY A BANKWIDE TEAM LED BY RUTH KAGIA AND comprising James Adams, Ian Bannon, Amar Bhattacharya, François Bourguignon, Xavier Coll, Roberto Daniño, Ian Johnson, Daniel Kaufmann, Michael Klein, Frannie Leautier, Mohamed Muhsin, Vikram Nehru, John Page, Gerard Rice, Jean-François Rischard, Jean-Louis Sarbib, John Wilton, and Shengman Zhang, with support from Andrew Follmer and Anne Joy Kibutu. The work was guided by a steering committee comprising James Adams, Caroline Anstey, Xavier Coll, Mohamed Muhsin, Gerard Rice, and Jean-Louis Sarbib. Produced in an unusually brief period of time, this publication would not have been possible without the exceptional responsiveness of the chapter authors and other credited contributors, the unwavering support and flexibility of the Bank's Office of the Publisher, or the incredible editorial and production work of Communications Development Incorporated.

In addition to the named authors, numerous staff contributed to the chapters and other content, including Elizabeth Adu, Kabir Ahmed, Ivar Andersen, Shaida Badiee, Christina Biebesheimer, John Briscoe, Sarah Cliffe, Anis Dani, Jean-Jacques Dethier, Michele Egan, Lucia Fort, Barbara Genevaz, Gita Gopal, R. Pablo Guerrero O., Kirk Hamilton, Tim Harford, Adnan Hassan, Dale Hill, Caroline Kende-Robb, Geoffrey Lamb, Bruno Laporte, Karen Mason, Soniya Mitra, Gobind Nankani, A. Waafas Ofosu-Amaah, Nadia Piffaretti, Carolyn Reynolds, Patricia Rogers, Cizuka Seki, Nina Shapiro, Sudhir Shetty, Warrick Smith, Anil Sood, Amy Stilwell, Susan Stout, Eric Swanson, Gregory Toulmin, John Underwood, and Linda Van Gelder. The team also appreciates the contributions from Angus Deaton, Amartya Sen, Nicholas Stern, and Joseph Stiglitz from the Chief Economist's Advisory Council.

Thanks go to Vivian Jackson for photo research and selection, with support from Deborah Campos, Patricia Davies, Anne Dronnier, Phillip Hay, Mukami Kariuki, Christina Lakatos, Dana Lane, Dale Lautenbach, Simone McCourtie, Sunetra Puri, Veronica Schreiber, Merrell Tuck, Nina Vucenik, and the team from the World Bank Archives. The team also thanks the following for their significant contributions beyond those already mentioned: Anis Dani, Annette Dixon, Eduardo Doryan, Robert Floyd, Shigeo Katsu, Michael Kubzansky, Anna Muganda, Marisela Montoliu Muñoz, Jose Augusto Palma, Praful Patel, Alexandra Tabova, Vinod Thomas, Nick Van Praag, and the Honorable Ngozi Okonjo-Iweala. Finally, the team would like to express its appreciation for the support received from Cathy Lamb and Anne Walsh.

Overview

BALANCING THE

DEVELOPMENT AGENDA

Because of Jim's leadership, the World Bank today is a more dynamic and effective development organization. I view his accomplishments as historic.

John Snow
U.S. Treasury Secretary
January 3, 2005

IN 1995 THE WORLD BANK WAS AN INSTITUTION UNDER SIEGE. NGOs criticized its environmental and structural adjustment policies, clients expressed dissatisfaction with its business approach, and the major shareholders showed frustration at its perceived inefficiency. Its 50-year celebrations in 1994 galvanized protest marches, crystallizing in the "50 years is enough" movement.

Criticism was wide ranging—from wasting taxpayers' money, to projects that ruined the environment, to policies that harmed people. The emerging antiglobalization movement that would persist through the 1990s helped fuel the attack on the Bank, deflecting public attention from the realities of poverty in the developing world.

Over the next 10 years the Bank changed significantly, becoming acknowledged once again, in many quarters, as the world's leading development agency. In September 2004 *The Economist* wrote: "The World Bank . . . does more to fight poverty than any other public body." How did this change happen? That is one of the questions this book seeks to answer. It brings together reflections of individuals closely associated with the changes in the Bank during the Wolfensohn years. In this sense it is a case study in institutional adaptation and regeneration.

Faced with questions about its relevance and effectiveness, the World Bank reshaped and refocused its mission, anchoring it on poverty reduction as the raison d'être of development. A rebalanced agenda has fundamentally altered the traditional relationships between the Bank and its clients and other partners. It has also changed the face of international development.

The reflections here portray the unique imprint of Jim Wolfensohn on the institution. He saw the Poverty War as a world war, which needed to be fought with the same passion and tenacity as the two World Wars and the

1995
James D. Wolfensohn Becomes the 9th World Bank President During a Period of Widespread Criticism of the Bank

Setting the Agenda
In his first Annual Meetings address, the new president outlines a strategic vision for the Bank: ensure that resources are sufficient to meet the needs of the world's poorest people, take an integrated approach to development, strengthen and expand partnerships, and develop further the institutional culture to focus on excellence and results.

1996
Cancer of Corruption
Wolfensohn's second Annual Meetings address identifies corruption as a barrier to development, the first time this issue is raised publicly by a senior World Bank official.

Cold War. He refocused the mission of the Bank on the global agenda. And by taking on rich country policies inimical to development—in such areas as aid, debt, and trade—he repositioned the Bank as an advocate for the poor.

I have learned that the real test of development can be measured . . . by the smile on a child's face.

James D. Wolfensohn
1995

Balancing the development agenda

In 1995 the Bank had to adjust to an emerging development paradigm that put poverty at the center of development efforts, recognizing equity as essential for prosperity and acknowledging the importance of institutions. This shift called for a reexamination of the Bank's core strategic thrust—against a backdrop of a world rapidly moving toward market-based democracies and globalization, fueled by the revolution in information and communications technologies.

In response, the Bank realigned the way it worked. It sharpened its focus on poverty reduction. It changed its relationship with the clients putting them in the lead. It broadened its reach and leverage by establishing or strengthening partnerships. It expanded the scope of its work to focus on binding constraints to poverty reduction. And it introduced far-reaching institutional changes that made it more responsive and more relevant. There were four elements to the change agenda: a new business model, declaring war on poverty, broadening the scope of Bank action, and realigning the institution.

A new business model

The Bank's new business model is undergirded by four principles:

- *People at the center* of the development effort. People are not spectators but central actors and the reason for development action. This principle is entrenched in the two-pronged strategy adopted by the Bank—investing in people and investing in growth.

1997

Renewal and Reorganization

The Strategic Compact is launched to improve the effectiveness of the Bank in its core mission of reducing poverty.

Putting the "R" Back in IBRD

Management presents to the Board a policy paper, "A Framework for World Bank Re-engagement in Post-Conflict Reconstruction," aimed at strengthening support for postconflict recovery, taking the institution back to its original mandate of reconstruction.

This is why the World Bank Group exists. . . To help make it happen for people.

James D. Wolfensohn
September 1997

- *Country-driven, comprehensive development.* The Comprehensive Development Framework (CDF) recognizes that all elements of the development process are interlinked and interdependent and cannot be addressed in isolation. The CDF and national poverty reduction strategies have restored the balance between national priorities and donor objectives while increasing the accountability of governments to their own societies. These strategies are owned by the developing countries themselves. They incorporate a comprehensive long-term vision bringing together structural, institutional, human, and macroeconomic aspects and identifying the links among them. They focus on outcomes. And they are participatory. In 2004, 42 low-income countries were implementing strategies guided by these features. Decentralization of the Bank has strengthened the country focus. By 2005, 73 percent of country directors were based in the field, compared with none in 1995.
- *Partnerships.* The Bank has become strategically networked with a range of partners, greatly increasing its leverage and outreach. Its global partnership program provides a financial channel for more than 600 bilateral donors and 100 international organizations. As an illustration, the Bank held $8.6 billion in trust funds in 2005.
- *Knowledge as a core strategy for reducing poverty.* Building on the revolution in information technology, the Bank has scaled up activities to make knowledge a key driver of development. It has put in place programs aimed at capturing and sharing knowledge within the institution and with clients. The programs include thematic communities of practice, advisory services, the Global Development Network, and the Development Gateway. The Shanghai conference in May 2004 acted as a

The Challenge of Inclusion

"Our goal must be to reduce these disparities across and within countries, to bring more and more people into the economic mainstream, to promote equitable access to the benefits of development regardless of nationality, race, or gender. This—the Challenge of Inclusion—is the key development challenge of our time."

—Jim Wolfensohn, Annual Meetings address, 1997

1998

A Bank That Stands on Two Legs

Wolfensohn uses his fourth Annual Meetings address to focus attention on "The Other Crisis"—the "human pain" that accompanied the Asian financial crisis—and heralds the need to focus on the structural and social issues key to long-term development.

global catalyst for creating, sharing, and applying cutting-edge knowledge for poverty reduction. It drew on more than 100 case studies from around the world, with lessons shared with 250,000 people through Web sites, 15–20 million through print media, and about 1.6 billion through television documentaries.

Declaring war on poverty

During his tenure Wolfensohn undertook more than 300 official trips to all regions of the world. On every trip he reiterated the need for faster and more comprehensive action on poverty reduction. He pushed rich countries to increase their support for development efforts. He urged poorer countries to improve their policies. To focus the message on poverty he crystallized it into four core parts, which he used in many of his speeches:

- *One world.* There are not two worlds, one rich and one poor. There is only one. We are linked in so many ways: not only by trade and finance, but also by migration, environment, disease, drugs, crime, conflict, war, and terrorism. We are linked—rich and poor alike—by a shared desire to leave a better world to our children, and by the realization that if we fail in one part of the planet, the rest becomes vulnerable. So poverty somewhere is poverty everywhere.
- *Global inequality, social justice.* The challenge of inclusion is the key development challenge of our time. In our world of 6 billion people, 1 billion own 80 percent of global GDP, while another billion struggle to survive on less than a dollar a day. In 2004 rich countries spent $56 billion a year on development assistance compared with $300 billion on agricultural subsidies and $600 billion on defense. Balanced

1999

Moving to a New Development Framework

The Bank launches a Comprehensive Development Framework, which emphasizes the interdependence of all elements of development.

Voices of the Poor

A landmark study based on consultations with 60,000 poor people in 60 countries reveals the human side of poverty and heightens the development community's understanding of poor people's view of poverty.

2000

Waging War on AIDS

In the first-ever address by a World Bank president to the UN Security Council, Wolfensohn calls for a war on AIDS.

Education for All

At the World Education Forum in Dakar, Senegal, the international community endorsed the Dakar Framework for Action to achieve universal primary education by 2015 and eliminate gender disparities in primary and secondary education by 2005.

development is in our self-interest—if we do not deal with poverty and social justice, we cannot have peace.

- *Hope.* Development works. The number of adults with no schooling has plummeted. Life expectancy in developing countries has soared. But the message of hope is best illustrated by the people the Bank serves—their strength, energy, and enterprise even in abject conditions.
- *The future.* In the next 25 years the global population will grow from 6 billion people to 8 billion, and more than 95 percent of the additional people will be in developing countries. By 2015 there will be 3 billion people under the age of 25. Our actions should protect their future.

Broadening the scope of Bank action

In the context of the broader definition of poverty, the Bank established new programs to address binding constraints to development. Combating corruption is now a core Bank program with 600 anticorruption programs in nearly 100 countries. Twenty-seven countries are receiving debt relief totaling $54 billion. As a way of leveling the playing field in the private sector, the Bank publishes the *Doing Business* reports, which benchmark the cost of business procedures in 145 countries. Contrary to past policy, Bank support is helping countries to remove user fees in primary education. The Bank's work in conflict countries has more than doubled to some 40 countries and territories.

The Bank also changed its relationship with the world. It strengthened its relationship with clients through the Comprehensive Development Framework, poverty reduction strategies, and decentralization. United Nations–Bank ties grew stronger, especially on such programs as AIDS, conflict, and

2001
A Millennial Challenge
The World Bank and the United Nations commit to the implementation of the Millennium Development Goals.

A Day of Remembrance
World Bank staff come together to remember those killed in the September 11 attacks.

2002
Development's Best Buy
The World Bank launches the Education for All Fast-Track Initiative to help developing countries meet the goal of universal primary education by 2015. It is the first effort to implement the Monterrey compact.

the environment. It reached out and engaged civil society organizations as partners in advocacy and implementation. Links with parliamentarians have grown through the Parliamentary Network, and the World Bank Institute has provided training for some 3,000 members of parliament from developing countries. The Bank developed links with leaders of more than 30 faith groups, premised on recognition that faith-based organizations are major actors on the ground, delivering more than one-third of education and health services in some of the poorest countries. More recently, the Bank has opened a global dialogue with the youth on issues such as employment and conflict.

Jim Wolfensohn leaves the Bank better equipped to fulfill the original ambitions of its founding fathers of combining powerful minds and noble motives in the cause of global partnership in an interdependent world.

Manmohan Singh
Indian Prime Minister
March 2005

Realigning the institution

To implement the new business model and remain responsive to a changing global environment, the Bank realigned and refocused the institution. It moved decisionmaking authority closer to the client through decentralization, made its products and services more client driven, put a premium on knowledge as a key driver of development, created incentives for technical excellence, and harnessed ICT to modernize business practices. The changes were underpinned by three pillars:

- *A matrix structure.* The establishment of a matrix structure has enabled the Bank to "think globally" through the network technical clusters and to "act locally" through country-driven programs. This structure has strengthened the Bank's ability to deepen its technical excellence and to tap into global knowledge and experiences, which are then applied as needed to country-specific situations.
- *A focus on results.* The need to manage for results by using information to improve decisionmaking and steer country-led development processes

2003
Cutting the Red Tape
Officials from donor and client countries meet in Rome for a forum on harmonization focused on streamlining the policies and procedures that guide delivery of development assistance.

2004
Scaling Up
The Shanghai Conference on Scaling Up Poverty Reduction brings the development community together to discuss actions to accelerate progress on poverty reduction.

Over the past 10 years that Jim has led the World Bank Group he has made the institution a beacon of hope and a true partner for developing countries working hard to improve the lives of their people. Jim stands out for his passion, enthusiasm, and boundless dedication to the cause of poverty eradication.

Olusegun Obasanjo
President of Nigeria
January 2005

toward clearly defined goals has become increasingly central to operational and aid effectiveness. The Bank has shifted from a project perspective to a country perspective and undertaken reforms to improve operational quality and to respond to specific development challenges as they arise.

- *Technical excellence and innovation.* Extensive human resources reforms have been undertaken to attract and retain the best possible global expertise and to foster learning and innovation. More than 800 managers were trained through the Executive Development Program.

The Bank has established incentives for excellence and innovation—for example, the Ideas Fund for Simplification supports simplification initiatives proposed by Bank staff. The fund can cover up to $30,000 of relevant expenses for winning ideas to streamline and improve any Bank process felt to be impeding the Bank's ability to deliver results in a timely and effective manner. Similarly, the Awards for Excellence program seeks to recognize outstanding team effort in serving clients. The Development Marketplace, launched in 1998, provides seed money for innovative development projects and allows the Bank to engage with social entrepreneurs.

This book outlines the key elements of the change agenda during Jim Wolfensohn's tenure under three headings: attacking poverty, leveraging through partnerships, and renewing the institution. This is followed by a discussion of some of the medium-term challenges likely to face the institution. To close the book, four leading development economists—Amartya Sen, Nicholas Stern, Joseph Stiglitz, and Angus Deaton—comment on Jim Wolfensohn's contributions to development.

2005
The Year of Development
2005 ushers in a year of unprecedented focus on development issues leading up to the Millennium Summit in September, with Sub-Saharan Africa set to dominate the G-8 Summit in July and a worldwide alliance of NGOs uniting to "make poverty history" through a Global Call to Action against Poverty.

May 2005
President Wolfensohn Retires

Part One

ATTACKING POVERTY

1

THE WORLD BANK'S DEVELOPMENT AGENDA HAS EVOLVED DRAMATICALLY IN the last 10 years—a decade of serious reevaluation of the development paradigm. There are five main areas of substantial progress:

- Making poverty reduction the objective of development.
- Adopting new instruments for development.
- Acknowledging the importance of institutions and governance.
- Seeing markets and states as complements.
- Recognizing equity and empowerment as essential for prosperity.

Making poverty reduction the objective of development

First of all, the Bank's agenda became more focused on the objective of poverty reduction. Indeed, the emphasis on poverty was not new. Development has long been concerned with improving living standards and reducing poverty. Only in the 1990s did poverty reduction become the overarching goal of development and development assistance.

What was new was that the emphasis on poverty reduction was fully articulated with growth, no longer antagonistic to it.

At the World Bank the change was spearheaded by the publication of the *World Development Report 1990* on poverty—with the first standardized global estimates of the prevalence of poverty—and by a strong shift in the institution's emphasis after the arrival of Jim Wolfensohn as president in 1995. Just as the Bank was adopting a new paradigm, it responded to the challenge of poverty reduction by gradually shifting to a new business model.

The accepted meaning of poverty reduction also began to change. In earlier decades, poverty was rather loosely defined as a particularly low level of income or consumption. In recent years, the development community has broadened

1996
The New Paradigm
In his address to the Board of Governors at the Annual Meetings, Jim Wolfensohn calls for a broader, more integrated approach to development, planting the seeds for the Comprehensive Development Framework.

1997
First HIPC Initiative Beneficiary
Uganda begins to receive debt relief as the first country to reach its decision point under the Heavily Indebted Poor Countries Initiative. On reaching the completion point a year later, Uganda qualifies for $650 million in total relief.

the meaning and objectives of development, with Amartya Sen particularly influential in persuading the development community to take such a broader view.

Poverty is now seen to include the inability to achieve standards rather than if they are actually achieved. People are defined as poor if they are unable to live the kind of life they value. Lacking adequate food or shelter, they also lack the education or health care that would permit them to live better. They are extremely vulnerable to illness, violence, economic dislocation, and natural disaster. They are poorly served by institutions of the state and society. And they often find themselves powerless to influence key decisions affecting their lives. Evidence has emerged to support this broader view. The World Bank's *Voices of the Poor,* which drew on interviews with some 60,000 poor people worldwide, shows that what poor people value in addition to higher consumption and income is access to opportunities, a secure social environment, freedom from violence, a voice in decisionmaking, and the power to hold others accountable for their actions.

The paradigm shift in the way we look at development that Jim Wolfensohn outlined on taking office has occurred, and he and the Bank have been a driving force in making it happen.

Hilde F. Johnson
Norway's Minister of International Development

The *World Development Report 2000/2001* clearly articulates the multifaceted dimensions of poverty, emphasizing that social development carries intrinsic value in addition to its instrumental value.

The Millennium Development Goals, adopted in 2000 and signed by 189 countries, signal this recognition and commit the development community to make progress in these multiple dimensions of poverty.

Adopting new instruments for development

A second area of progress was a gradual shift in instrumental approaches to development. What instruments should we use to reduce poverty? How would poverty reduction be achieved?

1998

"The Other Crisis"

In a preview of his Annual Meetings address later that year, Jim Wolfensohn emphasizes to participants at the G-8 Summit the need to deal with the social consequences of the Asian financial crisis, noting that Bank support should address social as well as financial dimensions.

Linking Governance and Aid Effectiveness

The Bank publishes *Assessing Aid: What Works, What Doesn't, and Why,* which argues that aid is more effective in countries that have good policies in place.

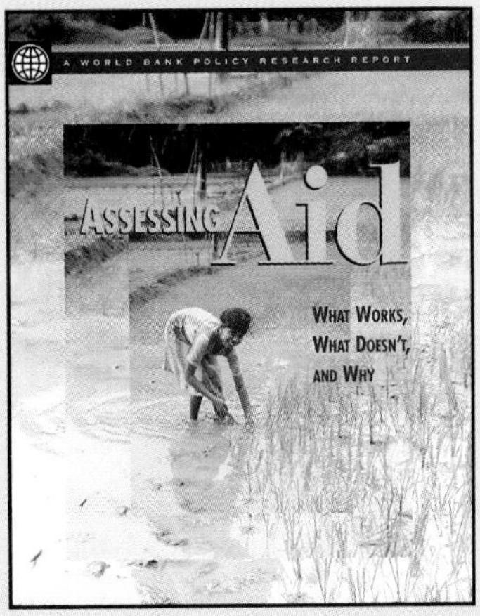

GENDER AND DEVELOPMENT

Jim Wolfensohn's presence at the 1995 Fourth World Conference on Women in Beijing, shortly after his appointment to the Bank, sent a strong signal to clients, development partners, and Bank staff that he considered achieving gender equality an integral element of development effectiveness. In Beijing, amid skepticism about the Bank's commitment to gender equality, he noted the achievements and remaining challenges associated with Bank assistance to education and health. He also promised that the Bank would work even more closely with its development partners to help realize the vision of economic advancement, justice, and opportunity for all women and men.

Wolfensohn has kept the promise he made in Beijing. Ten years later, he observes, "The last decade of innovation, experience, and activism has shown that improving women's and girls' lives is not a problem that has no solution; there are many practical steps that can be taken." One such step taken by the Bank was to make girls' education a corporate priority after Beijing, and to work closely with other partners in the global partnership for girls' education and the UN Girls' Education Initiative.

Under Wolfensohn's leadership, the decade since Beijing has witnessed several changes in the Bank. A Gender and Development Board was established to oversee the implementation of the gender agenda. An external Gender Consultative Group consisting of international experts was set up to provide feedback to the Bank. A Policy Research Report on gender marshaled a range of compelling evidence about the inextricable links between gender equality and poverty, reiterating that ignoring gender disparities comes at great cost to people's well-being and to countries' abilities to grow sustainably, to govern effectively, and thus to reduce poverty. After significant consultation with clients and other partners, a client-responsive gender policy was issued, and business procedures for implementation were established. The Bank also entered global and regional partnerships to catalyze the achievement of the Millennium Development Goals. The drive for gender equality was also reflected in the appointment of many women to management positions in the Bank, and women's voices began to be heard at all levels of the Bank's decisionmaking.

With strong institutional structures and systems in place within the Bank, gender issues are today increasingly being integrated into its country-level analytical work, lending operations, and policy dialogue. Most regions have conducted comprehensive gender diagnosis and analysis reports to help bring gender issues to the attention of policy makers. In addition, the Bank has completed Country Gender Assessments for nearly half its active client countries to help identify key gender inequalities that hinder economic growth and poverty reduction. Half of all poverty assessments completed in fiscal 2004 addressed gender issues in their analysis of poverty, and many proposed gender-responsive actions or policies to address gender inequalities.

This wealth of analytical work is also being reflected in the Bank's country strategies and lending—81 percent of the country assistance strategies approved in fiscal 2004 proposed gender-responsive actions to address inequalities in at least one sector. An assessment of lending projects approved showed that 81 percent of fiscal 2003 projects integrated gender issues in design, up from 69 percent over the previous two years.

Overall, these accomplishments illustrate significant progress in the decade since Beijing. The challenge will be to sustain the momentum in order to ensure that gender is fully mainstreamed into all levels of Bank assistance.

—A. Waafas Ofosu-Amaah and Sudhir Shetty

By the early 1990s the dominant approach to development economics was the "Washington consensus," which emphasized liberalization, privatization, fiscal discipline, openness to trade, protection of property rights, market-determined exchange and interest rates, and redirection of public spending toward education, health, and public infrastructure. A number of factors were responsible for the shift in instrumental approaches, including the relative failure of structural adjustment programs to contribute to growth and poverty reduction and the slow transition of countries of the former Soviet Union. And the Bank, through experience and trial and error, had gained a better understanding of what works. It then modified its approach to development and poverty reduction—reflecting the shift in the development community at large.

There is a clear understanding that unless inequalities between women and men in their access to resources and opportunity, rights, and voice are reduced, it will be difficult for the Bank to achieve its poverty reduction agenda.

External Gender Consultative Group

The Comprehensive Development Framework (CDF)—introduced by Jim Wolfensohn in 1999—provides a framework for development policy that integrates the economic and social aspects of development. The CDF represents an important move away from the excessive conditionality associated with adjustment lending programs. It promotes four principles:

- Development should be rooted in a long-term, holistic vision of a country's needs, focusing not just on macroeconomic aspects but also social and structural aspects.
- It should focus on results rather than inputs.
- It should be based on a country-owned strategy.
- Development actors should foster partnerships to support the country-owned strategy.

The main vehicle to implement the CDF was the poverty reduction strategy process, adopted by the World Bank and the IMF in 1999.

1999

Comprehensive Development Framework

The World Bank adopts the CDF to improve development effectiveness, with the first pilot in Bolivia launched in June 1999, and 12 more pilots launched over the next three months.

Putting the Client in the Driver's Seat

The World Bank and IMF adopt the approach of using the client-developed poverty reduction strategy as the basis for IMF, IDA, and HIPC Initiative support.

The Bank was orienting itself toward doing business in a medium-term perspective, moving away from ad hoc investment projects to program lending with adequate fiduciary safeguards and toward policy-consistent frameworks with clear targets for results and progress monitoring. It adopted a sharper focus on performance, and the CDF provided a clear monitoring framework to be discussed with governments and other donors. It also provided a vehicle for coordination and harmonization among donors.

The CDF recognized that the "Washington consensus" principles devoted too little attention to the policies needed to reduce poverty. Some of the principles, such as capital account liberalization and privatization, were too general. And they said nothing about governance and institutions, empowerment and democratic representation, country ownership for successful policy reform, or the social costs and pace of transformation—issues closely related to the political economy of reform.

It became clear that a "one-size-fits-all" policy package was counterproductive since development is specific to each country. The implication for development policy is that the key is to address the constraints to development at the right time and in the right way. In partnership with client countries and other donors, the Bank developed country assistance strategies tailored to specific country circumstances, based on two pillars: poverty reduction (with a broad, more inclusive view, stressing empowerment and effective service delivery) and growth and improvement of the investment climate.

Acknowledging institutions and governance

A third major element of the new development paradigm was the notion that societies with weak institutions have neither the software nor the hardware

2000
Attacking Poverty
The World Bank issues the *World Development Report 2000/2001: Attacking Poverty,* which expands the understanding of poverty and its causes—and outlines actions to create a world free of poverty in all its dimensions.

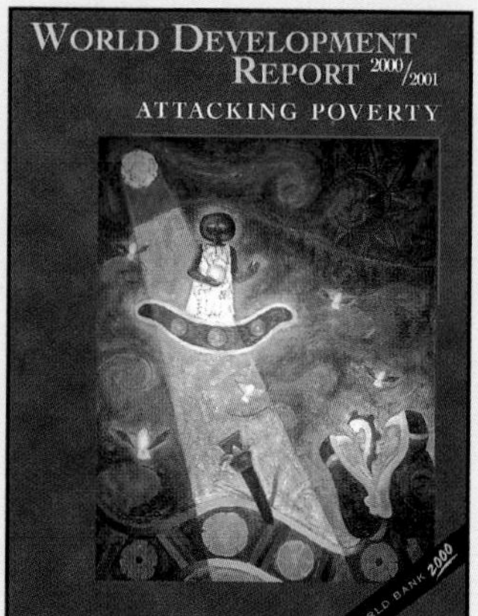

2001
Poverty Reduction as Global Security
Terrorist attacks and the heightened focus on global security underscore the importance of reducing poverty to peace and security.

for development. Weak institutions, poor governance, and corruption came to be viewed as an inequitable burden on citizens—and as a brake on economic growth that undermines incentives in the private sector. In the early 1990s many were skeptical of the impact and effectiveness of official development assistance. The influential 1998 study *Assessing Aid* provided evidence that foreign aid would have a greater impact on poverty reduction if it were focused on poor countries with stronger economic institutions and policies. The emphasis on governance and corruption, viewed as major obstacles to development, increased after 1996.

The Bank progressively increased country selectivity. By 2002 a country that improved its rating in the Bank's measure of policies and institutions, the Country Policy and Institutional Assessment (CPIA) index, by one standard deviation could expect to receive nearly 100 percent more in International Development Association (IDA) resources. Other donors have more recently increased their selectivity.

Within its mandate, the Bank is now focusing on operationalizing governance in various ways. First, through the CPIA and IDA rating process, the levels of development assistance to IDA countries now depend more on the quality of underlying governance and institutions, and less on policy commitments made by the recipient government. Second, the focus on public financial management has intensified because of the need to monitor the use of scarce funds for poverty reduction in countries under the Heavily Indebted Poor Countries (HIPC) Initiative. Third, many research reports—including the *World Development Report 2004* on service delivery, the *World Development Report 2005* on the investment climate, and the *Doing Business* reports—have contributed to increasing the awareness of the

2002
LICUS
The Low-Income Countries Under Stress Initiative is established to address the special challenges facing countries with very weak policies and institutions.

importance of institutions and governance in an operational development context.

Seeing markets and states as complementary

A fourth element of the new paradigm is the notion that markets and states are complementary mechanisms. The view that market and state are alternatives disappeared at the end of the Cold War. Now the almost universal consensus is that private enterprise, operating through the market, is the main engine of sustained economic growth—and that governments are essential to ensure that the investment climate is conducive to growth. The Bank started to carry out Investment Climate Assessments more systematically around 2001 to inform the policy dialogue and improve the design of reforms and assistance programs. The emphasis on sustainable growth led the Bank to reaffirm the importance of openness and international trade for poverty reduction. This translated into analytical work on policy, advocacy, and technical support for the World Trade Organization and the Doha negotiations.

Recognizing equity and empowerment as essential for the pursuit of prosperity

The fifth element of the new paradigm is that equity is essential for the pursuit of prosperity. A lack of equity—that is, inequality of opportunities—can slow the pace of poverty reduction. Inequitable societies are inefficient, and this perpetuates the cycle of low productivity and poverty. This is a departure from the simple prescription of achieving as much growth as possible and then redistributing its fruits.

2003

Making Services Work for the Poor

The World Bank launches the *World Development Report 2004* on how to improve delivery of basic services, one of the main challenges in the effort to eliminate poverty in our lifetime.

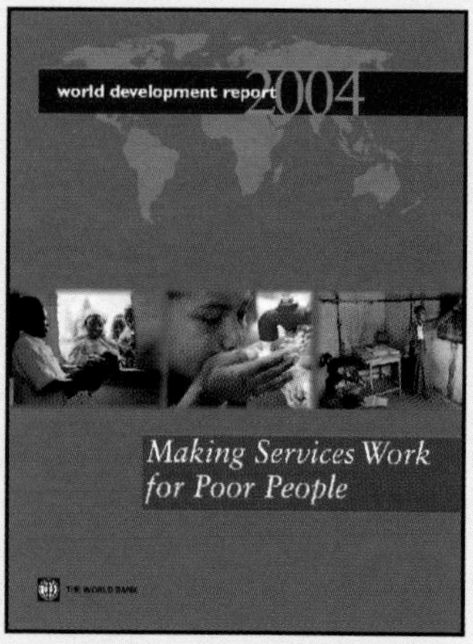

2004

Scaling Up in Shanghai

A global conference in Shanghai brings the development community together to discuss how to accelerate progress on the development agenda.

Equity and efficiency are complementary in some fundamental dimensions of development. In particular, promoting more equity is likely to generate faster sustained development. The long-run gain for society is likely to greatly exceed the short-run (efficiency) cost in promoting more equity. A key issue is to find mechanisms to guarantee that short-run losers in the promotion of equity will be more than compensated in the long run, so that a consensus to move out of the status quo and into reform can emerge.

Empowering people—ensuring that they can participate effectively in the economy and the society—is central to an effective development strategy. Empowerment, as both an end and a means of achieving other goals, influences other outcomes in many ways. Economic growth depends on a skilled and capable workforce, so empowering poor people to improve their health and education contributes to growth. Empowerment also increases a poor person's willingness and ability to take risks and innovate. And it contributes to improvements in governance.

Scaling up our development efforts

Barring an enormous increase in the pace of policy and institutional change in developing countries and in the external financing from rich countries, it is unlikely that most Millennium Development Goals will be reached in all regions by 2015. There is thus an urgent need to scale up our development efforts. The main directions for these efforts are known. The World Bank has shown leadership in responding to the challenges of poverty reduction in recent years. The reshaping of the Bank's role and approach in these areas has moved a long way, but the agenda is unfinished and needs sustained follow-through.

2004

Securing the 21st Century

In his final Annual Meetings address Wolfensohn highlights the fight to end poverty as the "challenge of our time," central to stability and peace.

2

IN HIS FIRST ANNUAL MEETINGS ADDRESS IN 1995, JIM WOLFENSOHN DESCRIBED his vision of lasting development as one that put people front and center. No longer viewed as mere spectators in the development process, people would have their own voice. They would express their own wishes and aspirations, and in doing so shape their own futures. This bold vision laid the foundation for human development to become a key priority for the Bank, a trend eventually reinforced by the unanimous adoption of the Millennium Development Goals (MDGs) by the world's leaders in September 2000.

Fighting "absolute" poverty had gained a new impetus from former World Bank president Robert McNamara's much-celebrated Nairobi speech in 1973. Jim Wolfensohn, in his decade at the helm of the Bank, went even further: he revitalized support for the social sectors, put a human face on the Bank's view of poverty, opened its doors to a vast new set of partners—including poor people—and maintained a steady emphasis on aiming for universal coverage of social services. Long viewed in technocratic and economic terms, the meaning of poverty changed to reflect the real struggles that poor people face in their daily lives. This more dynamic meaning of poverty demanded a definition that went beyond just measuring a dearth of incomes to encompassing notions of opportunity, inclusion, identity, culture, hope, empowerment, and dignity.

Broadening the reach of what it means to live in poverty allowed the establishment of a new development paradigm, which called for a holistic, comprehensive approach, with great emphasis on listening closely to the Bank's country clients and global partners, especially poor people.

Carrying out the new vision required action inside and outside the Bank. Internally, it meant articulating a strategy built on two pillars: investing in

1995
A Focus on People
In his first Annual Meetings address, Jim Wolfensohn outlines his vision of lasting development as one that puts people front and center, setting the stage to make human development a key priority for the Bank.

1997
Confronting AIDS
The World Bank launches *Confronting AIDS: Public Priorities in a Global Epidemic*, urging more intensive government prevention efforts to save lives and mitigate the economic and social costs of the epidemic.

and empowering people and improving the investment climate to spur growth. To implement the strategy, a new focus was placed on:

- Energizing the traditional social sectors (education, health, nutrition, population, and social protection).
- Developing new instruments that could accommodate and facilitate greater participation.
- Insisting that economic growth, while a vital component of reducing poverty, had to be balanced with efforts to make much-needed progress on human development outcomes. It also meant a research program highlighting the contribution of good human development outcomes to the investment climate and to growth.

Externally, it required amplifying the importance of human development in everything the Bank did, from Wolfensohn's speeches to a shift in the Bank's programmatic and lending priorities. It also meant partnering with those outside official government and donor channels to find the most effective means of reaching the most vulnerable. Crucial to shaping this agenda was the relentless repetition of these priorities—nowhere as evident and important as for Africa and for HIV/AIDS. The challenge was to keep promises and results at the top of the global development agenda, in the midst of crises and concerns more likely to create headlines, and to mobilize the attention of the world leaders, whether at Davos or the G-8 summits.

Education

Over the last 10 years, the evolution in the Bank's education work expanded to reflect the evolution in education worldwide. It has been characterized by five trends:

1998
Interfaith Dialogue
The meeting in Lambeth Palace, London, convened by Wolfensohn and the Archbishop of Canterbury, Dr. George Carey, is the first step in forging a partnership between the Bank and the world's faith communities around key issues of poverty alleviation and social justice.

1999
Voices of the Poor
A landmark study based on consultations with 60,000 poor people in 60 countries reveals the human side of poverty and heightens the development community's understanding of poor people's view of poverty.

- An increase in the volume of lending, restored to its highest level of $2.3 billion in 2004 after a dip to $800 million a few years before.
- Looking at the education sector in its entirety—from early childhood development to higher education—to ensure that each level benefits from and contributes to progress in the others. Cumulative lending for early childhood development grew from $800 million in 1995 to $1.5 billion in 2005, spread over 75 operations in 51 countries.
- A continuing emphasis on the importance of sending girls to school and reaching gender parity.
- A focus on quality and on the adaptation of education systems to local realities (especially in multilingual societies), and being competitive in a global economy.
- A drive to use information technology to accelerate progress—WorldLinks, the African Virtual University, and the Global Development Learning Network are examples.

These trends received a significant boost in 2000 at the World Education Forum in Dakar, Senegal, and with the adoption that same year of the Millennium Development Goals to achieve gender parity in 2005 and universal primary completion by 2015. To help reach the latter goal, at the request of the Development Committee in April 2002, the Bank launched the Education for All Fast-Track Initiative. Following the International Conference on Financing for Development in Monterrey, which established mutual responsibilities for rich and poor nations to reach the Millennium Development Goals, the Fast-Track Initiative represented a concrete effort to translate the Monterrey Consensus into practice.

2000

Education for All

The Dakar Framework for Action is adopted at the World Education Forum, reaffirming the international community's commitment to achieving Education for All by 2015.

GAVI Established

The Bank is a key partner in launching the Global Alliance for Vaccines and Immunization.

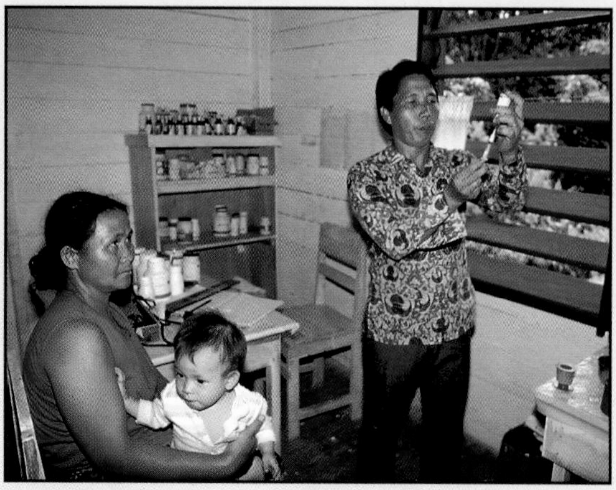

VOICES OF THE POOR—A LANDMARK STUDY

Poverty is pain; it feels like a disease. It attacks a person not only materially, but also morally. It eats away at one's dignity and drives one into total despair.

—A poor woman, Moldova

In March 2000 Jim Wolfensohn unveiled the first volume of the *Voices of the Poor* series, a groundbreaking study that presented, in their own words, the voices of 60,000 poor women and men from 60 countries around the world. By bringing the voices of poor people—who are the real poverty experts—to the policy world, the study changed the conceptualization of poverty and the strategies to fight poverty.

Speaking to leaders of poor people's organizations about the importance of the study and its findings, Wolfensohn said: "This attempt to reorient ourselves to actually link to the poor...was brought out in a way that has never been brought out by any institution; it gives the images of people in poverty, people who need voice, people who need a chance, people who are now part of the solution to the problems and not the object of charity...And into that fit the activities of our institution: first because we gave them voice with this study, and second because we care about it and we are working on it."

And work he did. The key messages from the study were included in his 1999 annual speech, even before the books were published. He worked tirelessly to communicate the key message from the study: poverty is multidimensional—it is about powerlessness and voicelessness; it is about violation of dignity, social isolation, widespread corruption, no recourse to justice, lack of protection from violence in the home, and hopelessness; and yet it is about resilience, resourcefulness, and solidarity. Poor people hunger most for a better future for their children.

Voices of the Poor had impacts that were both measurable and unmeasurable. The most important and difficult is for highly trained professionals to begin to see poor people as resources, to listen and to learn from them, and then to combine findings with technical expertise from the outside. The *World Development Report 2000/2001* carried a further message of empowerment to the world. This was followed by the development of the Bank's position on empowerment reflected in the *Empowerment and Poverty Reduction Sourcebook.*

The theme of inequality in power relations and its implications for institutional design and policies has moved forward in several ways, including a focus on the human rights framework, the role of voice and client power in making service work for the poor, and understanding the importance of inequality of agency and inequality of opportunity, the theme of the *World Development Report 2006* on equity.

A follow-up study—*Moving Out of Poverty: Understanding Growth, Freedom, and Democracy from the Bottom Up*—has been launched on an ambitious scale to understand once again from the bottom up how people move out of poverty, how they create wealth and prosperity, what factors help, and what factors hinder it.

—Deepa Narayan

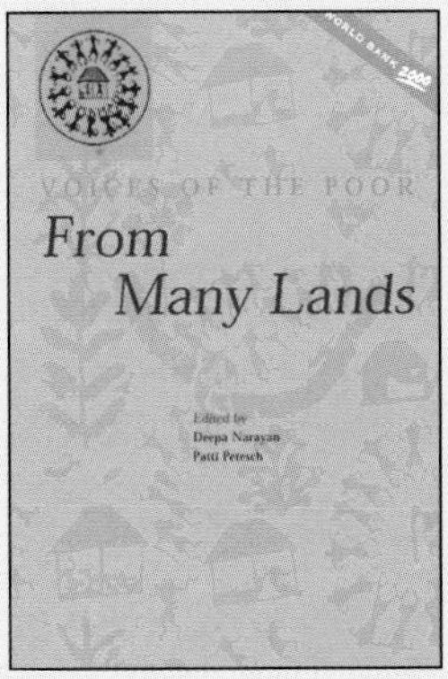

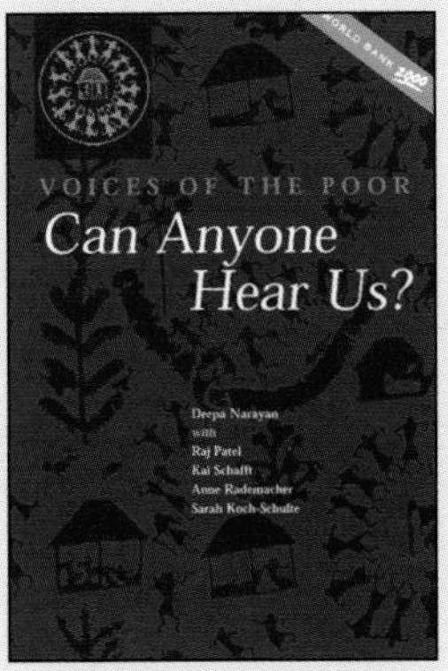

PURSUING THE MILLENNIUM DEVELOPMENT GOALS

The Millennium Development Goals (MDGs) summarize the commitments to sustainable development embodied in the Millennium Declaration, which was adopted unanimously by the 189 members of the United Nations in September 2000. Comprising 8 goals, 18 targets, and nearly 50 indicators and measuring progress from 1990 through 2015, the MDGs establish a yardstick for monitoring results, not just for developing countries, but for rich countries that help to fund development programs and for multilateral institutions that help countries to implement those programs. The World Bank has placed the MDGs at the center of its effort to fight poverty. For the international community, the MDGs represent an opportunity to demonstrate that development works when it is pursued within a coherent framework. For the more than 1 billion people living in extreme poverty, the MDGs represent a promise of a longer, healthier, and more productive life.

The MDGs

Goal 1	Eradicate extreme poverty and hunger
Goal 2	Achieve universal primary education
Goal 3	Promote gender equality and empower women
Goal 4	Reduce child mortality
Goal 5	Improve maternal health
Goal 6	Combat HIV/AIDS, malaria, and other diseases
Goal 7	Ensure environmental sustainability
Goal 8	Develop a global partnership for development

The MDGs were promulgated without an explicit agreement on how to finance them. The International Conference on Financing for Development in Monterrey, Mexico, in March 2002, was the first opportunity to address this problem. The consensus reached at Monterrey was framed as a compact of mutual accountability between developing and developed countries. Developing countries pledged to demonstrate their commitment to poverty reduction by improving their policies and governance. Rich countries agreed to provide more and better aid, increased access to their markets, and additional debt relief. The Monterrey compact provides a new framework of engagement between countries and their development partners. For example, the MDGs increasingly form the basis for the design of monitoring targets in Poverty Reduction Strategy Papers. The regional development banks have adopted a new, results-based approach closely linked to the MDGs. And the European Union and many bilateral donors have reoriented their aid effort toward meeting the Goals, in many cases making them the main focus of all their work.

Now at their five-year mark, there is evidence of progress toward the Goals, but the pace has been uneven and on average too slow to ensure that many countries will achieve them. Faster progress is possible, as some of the better performing regions and countries have demonstrated. But there is no simple, quick fix that will guarantee success. What is needed now is concerted action within the framework of enhanced global development partnership envisaged at Monterrey. The large-scale review of the MDGs undertaken by the United Nations Millennium Project in collaboration with the World Bank and many other agencies concluded that more resources, coherent policies, and faster growth are needed to achieve the Goals. In this spirit, the *Global Monitoring Report 2005* proposes a five-point agenda for accelerating progress toward the MDGs:

- Anchor actions to achieve the MDGs in country-led development strategies.
- Improve the environment for stronger, private-sector-led economic growth.
- Scale up delivery of human development services.
- Dismantle barriers to trade.
- Substantially increase the level and effectiveness of official development assistance.

None of this will be easy. But much depends upon it.

—Eric V. Swanson

Health, nutrition, and population

In his view of globalization, Jim Wolfensohn often mentioned health as yet another link making the world "one." Together with his strong call for partnerships, this led the Bank to take a leading role in the development of global programs to address issues and diseases that know no borders. The Onchocerciasis [river blindness] Control Programme provided a good model: public and private actors worked together with local communities and NGOs to make remarkable progress toward eradicating a disease that affected millions of people and forced entire villages in West Africa to move away from fertile lands near rivers.

Building on this model of participation and partnership, the Bank was active in launching the Roll Back Malaria program and the Stop TB partnership, and was one of the founding members of the Global Alliance for Vaccines and Immunization (GAVI). To facilitate the inclusion of such global initiatives in country programs, a strong effort was made to provide evidence of the impact of disease on economic and social development. And new financial instruments were developed allowing Bank partners to reduce the cost of borrowing for tuberculosis or polio vaccinations. Similar efforts at partnering led to contacts and bridge-building with the pharmaceutical industry, for brand-name and generic drugs.

Attacking HIV/AIDS

With its seemingly relentless and deadly march across countries and continents, the AIDS pandemic has become the major development challenge in Sub-Saharan Africa and the Caribbean, killing workers in the prime of life, reducing life expectancy, leaving millions of orphans in its wake, and

2001

A Millennial Challenge

The World Bank commits itself as a full partner to the United Nations in the implementation of the Millennium Development Goals.

Global Plan to Stop TB

The World Bank and the World Health Organization launch the Global Plan to Stop TB—more than 120 groups join to control and eventually eliminate tuberculosis.

No money can replace leadership at all levels.

Peter Piot
Executive Director, UNAIDS
November 2003

jeopardizing long-term growth prospects. It now threatens to expand rapidly to India, China, Russia, and Eastern Europe.

The Bank's reaction, slow to start, has broadened and accelerated since 1995, and Jim Wolfensohn has been a strong and consistent leader: breaking taboos, fighting stigma, advocating for action, and demanding results.

The Bank has become a major source of funding for AIDS in Africa and the Caribbean, committing more than $1 billion through the Multi-Country HIV/AIDS Program. Focused on implementation challenges, the program is reaching out to communities, simplifying procedures, and creating a network of professionals specialized in fighting HIV. The Bank has worked with communities and countries to procure cheaper and effective antiretroviral drugs and has entered agreements with the Clinton Foundation to reduce their price.

The challenge today is not only to mobilize additional financing above and beyond the progress already made (with funding having grown from $300 million 10 years ago to $6 billion in 2004), but to close the growing implementation gap and to ensure that the countries are in a position to strengthen their health systems to address prevention, care, and treatment. The challenge is also to address the growing feminization of the epidemic and to take action to ensure equal protection and care for men, women, and children.

Protecting the most vulnerable

The protection of the most vulnerable people has been one of the central themes of Wolfensohn's tenure, reflected, in part, in the growth in lending for social protection from $1.5 billion in 1995 to $2.5 billion in 2005. It meant deepening our focus on the social consequences of economic and

2002

Mainstreaming Gender

The World Bank launches its Gender Mainstreaming Strategy, aiming to work with governments and civil society in client countries and with other donors to reduce gender-related barriers to development and capitalize on opportunities for poverty reduction and sustainable development.

Development's Best Buy

The World Bank announces that 23 countries will be invited to join the Education for All Fast-Track Initiative to help developing countries meet the Millennium Development Goal of universal primary education by 2015.

structural reforms, and targeting scarce public expenditures more effectively to reach those who need them most.

To provide Bank clients and staff with the tools and knowledge to protect vulnerable groups in society, the social protection family developed products and evidence-based policy recommendations in a variety of fields: safety nets, labor market analysis, income support for workers during transition and unemployment periods, social funds to empower communities. It also introduced the dynamic concept of vulnerability to shocks as a way to deepen poverty analysis.

Being more inclusive

The driving force was the challenge of inclusion. To fight poverty and to meet the Millennium Development Goals, the Bank would have to adopt an inclusive approach, reaching out to the excluded and the marginalized, be they commercial sex workers, lower castes, malnourished children, child soldiers, people living with the stigma of AIDS, or the vast number of women too poor and too marginal to have their voices heard and their needs taken into account. Jim Wolfensohn never failed to remind audiences that these people were not only the true clients of the Bank, but that they were also the bearers of long-term solutions. Three examples illustrate this approach: people with disabilities, the Roma, and youth.

People with disabilities. Six hundred million people in the world live with some form of disability. Most disabled people are poor. Clearly, special attention needs to be given to their situation if results matter in the fight against poverty, yet these people remained mostly invisible in our analysis of

2002

Disability and Development

The Bank appoints its first Advisor on Disability and Development. Informal discussions at the World Bank during the December celebration of the UN International Day of Disabled Persons lead to the establishment, a year later, of the Global Partnership on Disability and Development.

MDG Financing Gap

At the Monterrey Conference on Financing for Development, Wolfensohn rallies donor pledges in response to the need for an additional \$40–\$60 billion a year to achieve the Millennium Development Goals.

Throughout his tenure he has worked tirelessly and with incredible dedication to use the Bank's power to alleviate poverty around the world. I have been particularly impressed by his deep personal commitment to an issue that is close to my heart, the plight of the Roma people in Europe.

George Soros
Founder and Chairman
Open Society Institute

poverty. The appointment of a special adviser on disability helped throw light on the issue and allowed Bank staff and other organizations to discover the potential for progress in partnering with organizations focusing on people with disabilities. Simple solutions can make a difference: in the Brazilian census, a simple question on visual acuity identified millions of children needing reading glasses and transformed their ability to learn in school.

The Roma. With the European Union enlargement in May 2004, the Roma became the largest minority in Europe, at 7 million to 9 million. One of the fastest-growing populations on the continent, the Roma are also the most vulnerable. Conditions for many Roma in Central and Eastern Europe deteriorated with the transition from socialism in the 1990s. They were often the first to be laid off from jobs and have been among those most persistently blocked from reentering the labor force. Many Roma have limited opportunities because of low education and health status, long-standing exclusion, and the inability to participate in social and political life.

Together with George Soros and his network of Open Society Institutes, the Bank convened the first high-level conference on Roma in Central and Eastern Europe in 2003 in Budapest, Hungary. For the first time, prime ministers and other senior government officials from eight countries came together with Roma leaders to discuss strategies for overcoming exclusion and expanding opportunities for Roma to contribute to economic and social development in Europe.

2003

Inclusion of Civil Society

As part of the Annual Meetings, Wolfensohn participates in a town hall meeting with civil society organizations, joined by IMF managing director Horst Kohler and key finance officials from around the globe.

Bringing Europe's Most Vulnerable Minority into Society

Launch of the Decade of Roma Inclusion and the Roma Education Fund, to reduce poverty among Roma and include them in European society through better education, health care, housing, and job opportunities.

Youth. The Bank's "success" will rest on its ability to provide a safe and secure future for the children and youth of today. Children and youth represent nearly half the world's population and the majority of the developing world's poor are under 25. More than a billion of them will need jobs in the next decade.

Wolfensohn's emphasis on the importance of listening to the perspectives of young people has affected the way the Bank is meeting the complex challenges facing this group. Since 2000 there has been a sharp increase in the number of projects, in the overall lending amounts, and in the number of sectors focusing on addressing the challenges facing youth, including youth employment, risky behavior, skill building, and empowerment. Two conferences on Youth, Development, and Peace in 2003 and 2004 have helped to build bridges with youth organizations and start a dialogue on how best they can contribute today to the elaboration of policies that affect them.

At the height of the structural adjustment years, critics of the Bank demanded "adjustment with a human face." Today, human development is at the center of the Bank's activities. After a decade of Jim Wolfensohn's leadership, the Bank has been transformed into a true, credible, and respected partner in the fight to build a better and more equitable world for all.

2004

Making HIV/AIDS Drugs Affordable

The World Bank joins the Global Fund, UNICEF, and the Clinton Foundation in announcing agreements that will make it possible for developing countries to purchase high-quality AIDS medicines and supplies at the lowest available prices.

Collaborating with Youth

Wolfensohn travels to Sarajevo for the second conference on Youth, Development, and Peace to gather input from representatives of more than 100 youth organizations on development issues and identify opportunities for further cooperation between youth organizations and the World Bank.

3

MOST PEOPLE NOW ACCEPT THAT ECONOMIC GROWTH IS FUELED BY THE PRIVATE sector, which also creates the majority of jobs and lifts people out of poverty. But over the past 10 years, the key reforms advocated to promote growth have changed. In the mid-1990s macroeconomic stabilization was high on the agenda: countries were encouraged to nail down inflation and increase the savings rate. Those days were also the heyday of privatization, with huge utility sell-offs in Argentina and voucher privatization schemes in the former Soviet Union. Financial market liberalization was widespread, too—for example, the number of emerging markets that had liberalized their current accounts more than doubled between 1991 and 1996. With the IMF campaigning on the macroeconomic front, the World Bank took a leading role in helping to structure the privatization of utilities and private participation in other infrastructure. The World Bank has not abandoned privatization, but its remit for helping the private sector promote development is now much broader.

Today, macroeconomic stabilization and privatization are no longer regarded as sufficient to promote growth. Expert opinion has changed—for example, Mexico's crash of 1994 was widely blamed on a low domestic savings rate and consequent overdependence on foreign funds. Yet when the high-savings-rate economies of East Asia went through their own crises, it became clear that microeconomics mattered too.

The Asian crisis was not the only stumble along the way. Private participation in infrastructure became less popular: users protested against having to pay for services that had previously been free, governments fretted about the political costs, and private firms were discouraged by low returns and the risks posed by the controversy. Many people were disheartened by the

The Engine for Growth and Poverty Reduction
A vibrant private sector is now widely understood to be the engine for growth and sustainable poverty reduction. Supporting this goal is now the subject of a unified World Bank Group Private Sector Development Strategy.

situation in the former Soviet Union, especially in the wake of the ruble crisis: privatization had not created market institutions quickly, nor prevented a collapse in the Russian economy. Russia had the oligarchs; Asia, "crony capitalism." And even in the developed world the dot-com bubble and corporate governance scandals at Enron, WorldCom, Parmalat, and the rest made people less willing to trust the private sector.

Privatization and macroeconomic stability not enough for growth

The lessons of the 1990s were that privatization and macroeconomic stability could not by themselves create thriving economic growth. Competition was important: a privatized monopoly was no better than a state-owned monopoly. Entrepreneurs needed to be free to set up new firms, free to grow, and free to fail—which meant appropriate business regulation. Corporate governance mattered, and so did corporate social responsibility. All in all, the importance of the private sector for development had not changed: it had simply become apparent that private sector development was a more subtle business than was appreciated in the 1990s.

Jim Wolfensohn recognized these new subtleties in the Comprehensive Development Framework, and he provided the World Bank Group with the capability to respond when he decided for the first time to combine the role of executive vice president of the International Finance Corporation (IFC) with that of managing director responsible for private sector development and infrastructure in the Bank. This allowed the World Bank Group to formulate a unified strategy for private sector development. The new

2000
Joining Forces
The joint World Bank–International Finance Corporation global product groups are created for telecommunications, oil, gas, mining, and advisory services.

strategy acknowledged the complexity of the conditions for a thriving private sector, and decisively shifted the agenda away from a focus on privatization and toward the broader area of investment climate reform.

Leveling the playing field

The big challenge now is to level the playing field for responsible business. In too many countries, businesses operate at a disadvantage because they are too small to cope with burdensome regulations, or because they are trying to maintain standards where competitors flout them, or because they pay taxes and others do not, or because they are owned by foreigners or minority groups. These problems are not only morally objectionable—they are damaging for economic growth and for poor people.

The joint World Bank–IFC *Doing Business* reports produce objective, intuitive measures of the cost of common business procedures in 145 countries—such as collecting payment from a recalcitrant customer, registering a new business, or buying commercial property. Poor countries tend to have much more costly and time-consuming regulations than rich ones, and these overly burdensome regulations extract a heavy toll by slowing down economic growth. Competitive pressures become less effective: less efficient informal firms can hold their own against more efficient formal firms that respect regulations and pay taxes.

Worse, the regulations hurt those that they are supposed to help. For example, employment protections are correlated with the disappearance of women from the labor force. The poor and the excluded end up in the informal sector with worse jobs and no effective rights.

2003
Doing Business
The Bank launches its first *Doing Business* report, detailing objective measurements of the regulatory burden in more than 130 countries, revealing that poor countries regulate most heavily, and gathering together the information necessary for simple reforms.

2004
***WDR* on Investment Climate**
Launch of the *World Development Report 2005: A Better Investment Climate for Everyone,* highlighting the critical role of the investment climate. This is the first *WDR* to focus on private sector development—and is heralded by the *Financial Times* as "the most important report the Bank has ever produced."

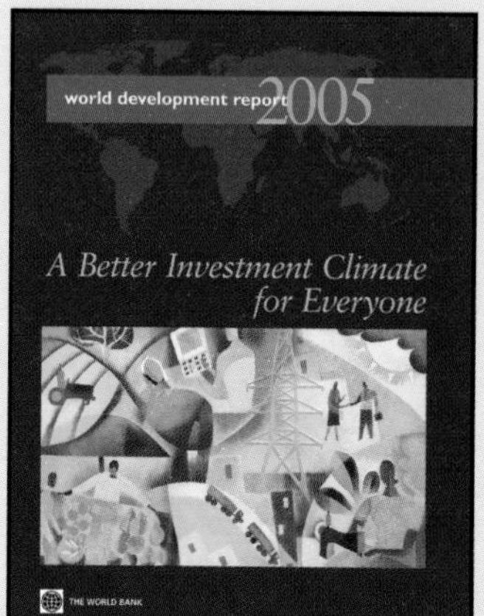

The World Bank's work is continuing to uncover these insights to help develop clear, locally tailored strategies for reform and to provide the data to advance our understanding. The Doing Business project, picked up in hundreds of newspapers worldwide, posts on the Internet all its time-and-motion data, plus its vast database of local laws and regulations. These resources are beginning to be used by academics and reformers alike. Similarly, the online Investment Climate Survey database provides a rich set of data based on responses from over 27,000 firms. Meanwhile, the agenda-setting *World Development Report 2005,* praised by the *Financial Times* as "the most important report the World Bank has ever produced," pulled together the state of the art on investment climate reform.

Finding systems that work

Economic growth requires not just the "soft" infrastructure of efficient regulation and the rule of law, but the more familiar "hard" infrastructure of roads, power, telecommunications, and safe water. For political reasons, among others, it is often difficult to accept a laissez-faire solution to these problems: people may be willing to pay enough to cover the cost of mobile phone calls, but in many parts of the world it is hugely unpopular to ask users to pay the true cost of safe water, for instance. Nevertheless, somebody must pay in the end—whether users, taxpayers, or a combination of the two. So the World Bank has adopted a pragmatic and flexible approach, working with governments to find systems that work, whether public, private, or a mixture.

There is a role for the private sector in infrastructure provision, but it is most effective with well-targeted government support. Too often in the past,

Output-Based Aid

The World Bank Group is pioneering new ways of combining public financing with private sector delivery of public services to improve targeting of subsidies while sharpening incentives for performance. The initial pilot projects include those to extend piped water services in rural Cambodia.

subsidized public utilities have delivered cheap water and power only to the well connected, while the poor have missed out and have had to pay black market prices for essential services. Now "output-based aid" or "performance-based subsidies" are targeting subsidies directly at the poor, using a competitive procurement process to harness the efficiency of the private sector while shielding the poor from the full cost of being connected to water or electricity systems. The World Bank Group is currently pursuing about 30 such schemes.

Working directly with private businesses

The IFC and MIGA (Multilateral Investment Guarantee Agency) are also working directly with private businesses. It is one thing for the Bank Group to help create a good environment for doing business—it is another for businesses to recognize this and be comfortable investing in unfamiliar developing countries. So the IFC and MIGA support and reassure private businesses—the IFC by coinvesting with private banks, and MIGA by insuring projects against political risks. Recently, the IFC has rapidly increased its investment in emerging markets. Tremendous opportunities can be unlocked by the simple process of demonstrating that a project made money where previously investors feared to tread.

The IFC provides other support to businesses. For example, IFC technical assistance programs to domestic banks are providing them with tools and techniques for lending to small businesses, creating value for the banks and the small businesses alike. And the IFC has been a leader in the field of corporate responsibility. Its strategy is founded on the belief that responsible business practices are not a pointless expense, but a valuable asset for the

A Unified World Bank Group Approach

The International Finance Corporation

Working with business partners, the IFC invests in sustainable private enterprises in developing countries without accepting government guarantees. It provides equity, long-term loans, structured finance, risk management products, and advisory services. In addition to finance, the IFC adds value to projects through its corporate governance, environmental, and social expertise.

IFC International Finance Corporation World Bank Group

The Multilateral Investment Guarantee Agency

MIGA helps promote foreign direct investment in developing countries by providing guarantees to investors against noncommercial risks and by providing technical assistance and advisory services to governments.

MULTILATERAL INVESTMENT • GUARANTEE AGENCY • M.I.G.A.

business itself and for society. Yet it is not always easy for businesses to know how best to behave, especially when dealing with new markets. The IFC is trying to develop a competitive strength based on the quality of its advice in the area of corporate responsibility. It also built on this strength in 2003, when major private investment banks (responsible for 80 percent of project finance in emerging markets) jointly agreed to sign up to the IFC's environment and social standards, under the banner of the Equator Principles.

Laying the foundations for economic growth

What lies ahead? Despite a fall in flows of foreign direct investment in recent years, it seems likely that private sector financial flows will continue to increase in importance. Remittances, private equity, and nonsovereign debt have all expanded over the past 20 years, even leaving aside the recent boom and bust. There seems to be plenty of room for further expansion, too: many countries continue to miss out. Eventually, it seems likely that they will create the business environment to attract foreign investment and stimulate domestic enterprise.

It is not too far-fetched to speculate that in 15 or 20 years, we will find that business-environment reform has gone the way of fiscal rectitude and the control of inflation: universally accepted as a priority, solved in the majority of countries. After all, many investment climate problems are technically straightforward and are politically easier to address than cutting spending and raising taxes.

Foreign Direct Investment—An Important Part of the Story

Despite recent booms and busts in FDI flows to developing countries, it seems likely that private sector financial flows will continue to increase in importance as an engine for development.

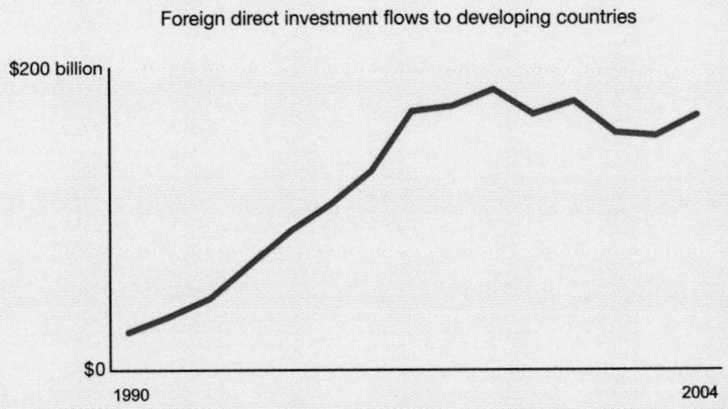

INTEGRATING INNOVATIVE FINANCE INTO IFC'S OPERATIONS

One major challenge facing the International Finance Corporation (IFC) in recent years has been to provide innovative financial solutions that fit client needs in emerging and transition markets and that stimulate development of capital markets. This needs to be accomplished while preserving capital and ensuring that funds remain available as needed for IFC's private sector investments in developing countries.

IFC's Treasury and Vice Presidency of Finance has taken up the challenge. The focus has been on financial innovation that integrates structured finance and derivative products into IFC's operations, as well as makes local currency lending in emerging markets more of a reality. Chapter 15 further discusses World Bank Group financing instruments. IFC has become the leader in the market and among other supranationals in setting up local currency structures. These efforts have established an in-house investment bank that makes a key contribution to IFC's mission of supporting the sustainable development of the private sector in emerging markets.

Today IFC, as the private sector arm of the World Bank Group, can offer a wide range of sophisticated financial products that contribute to its competitiveness as well as its development objectives.

Structured finance

IFC has been at the forefront of domestic capital market development, placing special emphasis on creating structured products to enable these markets to grow. Through its active participation in the structuring and credit enhancement of transactions, IFC has helped introduce new asset classes in markets around the world. The transactions have not only enabled IFC's clients to secure attractive, long-term local currency financing; they have also been catalysts for expansion of numerous domestic markets.

IFC's operations in structured finance focus on structuring partial credit guarantees and securitizations in a way that will be sustainable for actively developing local markets. Efforts particularly target mortgage finance, small and medium enterprises, and financial institutions. Especially notable transactions include securitizations to initiate or expand mortgage finance in the Baltic states, Colombia, the Republic of Korea, Mexico, and South Africa; guarantees for subordinated bonds involving Tier 2 capital in Colombia and Brazil; a guarantee for a bond to introduce Compartamos, a Mexican microfinance company, to the capital markets; risk-sharing facilities for education in Africa and Latin America; a guarantee for a municipal bond in Johannesburg and a partial credit guarantee to finance a municipal water project in Mexico; the first nonperforming loan securitization in the emerging markets; and guarantees for bonds and loans in the manufacturing, telecommunications, agribusiness, health, education, and insurance sectors in Latin America, Asia, and Africa.

A special initiative is under way with the rating agencies to develop guarantee facilities that will allow IFC to be particularly efficient in local currency lending. Treasury's emphasis on the use of partial guarantees for credit-enhancing transactions has resulted in a significant leveraging of IFC's resources. It is notable that in the last few years, about $500 million in IFC exposure has resulted in approximately $3 billion in market financing. Structured transactions are being completed at the rate of one or two a month and the pipeline continues to grow.

Derivative products and risk hedges

IFC is one of the few organizations able to bridge the credit gap and extend long-maturity risk management products to clients in emerging markets. It does this by intermediating derivatives as hedges for currency, interest rate, or commodity price exposure. Also using the derivative market, IFC has been able to provide direct loans in local currency, which is critical for companies that need to match the currency of their revenues. These products have been transacted in over 30 countries, and IFC has disbursed more than $1 billion in local currency loans and hedges.

Local currency lending using derivatives continues to grow, as IFC uses its swap market relationships to extend the maturity of derivatives markets in additional countries. In late 2004 and early 2005, about $200 million in local currency loans were disbursed in India, Mexico, South Africa, and Thailand. IFC also executed hedging instruments for a total of $50 million in

Kenya and Peru, and the Corporation is working with a Russian gold-mining client to provide a gold-indexed loan. As exposure in such derivatives and hedges has grown, IFC's investment officers have improved their understanding of the benefits of risk hedging for clients.

Among notable transactions, in early 2005 IFC obtained approval from the Brazilian authorities to undertake swaps in the local market, where IFC is developing a synthetic swap guarantee structure. In 2004, IFC disbursed and structured several ruble-indexed loans to financial institutions in Russia, taking advantage of the offshore hedging market to provide ruble financing synthetically. In Vietnam, IFC is developing long-term loans denominated in Vietnamese dongs, with the currency hedge sourced from two international banks. In China, IFC is developing renminbi-indexed loans to meet the local currency needs of clients.

Funding

IFC has been proactive in opening emerging capital markets, both by functioning as a pioneer foreign issuer and by helping to establish regulations and practices that help stimulate these markets. While all supranationals share this objective—and have a special significance and arbitrage advantage in initial issuance—IFC is particularly suited to this role because of its focus on the private sector.

Since the mid-1980s IFC has borrowed in 31 currencies, many from countries that were emerging capital markets at the time IFC first borrowed. Emerging capital markets have always been an important part of the Corporation's borrowing program, for a variety of reasons. In many cases, when countries first open their capital markets, they prefer to do so by letting supranational institutions in which they are members be the first borrowers. IFC client companies in developing countries also benefit from broader access to local funding that a deeper market offers in terms of maturity.

These transactions not only have helped develop capital markets and diversify IFC's own investor base, but also have helped establish IFC's own credit, particularly in domestic markets where the valuation of an IFC benchmark is established. This has been particularly important as IFC has become more proactive in developing local currency instruments and enhancements through structured finance. In effect, IFC's effort to open domestic markets has also helped establish IFC's credit among domestic investors, and it has facilitated the further introduction of local currency structured products.

Since 2000 IFC has been the inaugural foreign issuer in the domestic public market for Colombian pesos, Moroccan dirhams, Peruvian soles, and Singapore dollars (the Colombian and Moroccan transactions were also the first supranational domestic issues in their respective regions). With a Malaysian ringget issue, IFC recently issued the first supranational Islamic bond in any local currency.

By accelerating the development of the emerging capital markets, IFC is enabling more and more companies based in developing countries to access domestic capital through the issuance of bonds in their own currency.

—Nina Shapiro

4

IN DECEMBER 1999 THE BOARDS OF THE WORLD BANK AND THE INTERNATIONAL Monetary Fund approved a new approach to their relations with low-income countries, based on country-owned poverty reduction strategies. The approach—centered on the Poverty Reduction Strategy Paper (PRSP)—was in many ways novel. It made the successful preparation of a nationally owned poverty reduction strategy, as detailed in the PRSP, a precondition for access to debt relief and concessional financing from both institutions. The strategies were expected to be poverty focused, country driven, results oriented, and comprehensive. They were also expected to serve as a framework for better coordination of development assistance among other development partners.

While the PRSP was a joint operational approach of the Bank and the Fund, it was fundamentally the descendant of the Comprehensive Development Framework, introduced by Jim Wolfensohn in January 1999. That framework, which the Bank had begun to pilot in 13 low- and middle-income countries, had four key elements that would become hallmarks of the PRSP. Wolfensohn argued that successful development strategies should:

- Be owned by developing countries themselves, with the goals, timing, and sequencing of programs to realize them determined in line with each country's unique needs and capabilities.
- Incorporate a comprehensive, long-term vision, bringing together structural, institutional, human, and macroeconomic aspects of the development process—and identifying the links among them.
- Build a participatory, partnership-based approach to realizing the vision, involving governments, national stakeholders (including civil society), and external partners in a cooperative effort with shared goals and responsibilities.

1995
Planting the Seeds for CDF
The new president uses his first Annual Meetings address to call for a more integrated approach to development.

1999
Adoption of PRSPs
The World Bank and IMF adopt nationally owned participatory poverty reduction strategies as the basis for all World Bank and IMF concessional lending.

- Focus on development outcomes, setting out the links between overall aims and the practical actions needed to progress toward them and identifying clear, monitorable indicators of progress.

The PRSP reflected three important trends in thinking about development and development assistance that emerged in the 1990s. First, development agencies in the rich countries, including the Bank and the Fund, felt the need to frame the political debate over aid and debt relief in more human terms. Strategies for poverty reduction provided an appropriate, people-centered development objective. Second, the academic research on aid effectiveness had clearly demonstrated that processes of economic change not owned by the societies trying to implement them did not succeed in the long run—hence the emphasis on country ownership embedded in the PRSP process. And third, the aid community was paying more attention to the benefits of involving stakeholders, including beneficiaries, in the design and implementation of development projects and programs. PRSPs were thus to be produced using participatory methods.

The CDF created an environment where the Bank directly supported the Ugandan government's Policy Eradication Action Program, moved to a lending program that included substantial budget support and actively utilized Uganda's own capacity to develop and implement projects and programs.

Emmanuel Tumusiime
Governor
Central Bank of Uganda

Today, 43 low-income countries are implementing their poverty reduction strategies, and 23 have been doing so for more than one year. As implementation has progressed, the poverty reduction strategy approach has resulted in important changes in the way low-income countries, the Bank, the IMF, and other development partners approach development.

Perhaps the most significant contribution of the PRSP process is to have reaffirmed the centrality of country ownership of development policy. It helped restore the balance between national priorities and donor objectives, while increasing the accountability of governments to their own societies. Parliaments are now more regularly engaged in PRSP formulation and

2000
First Interim PRSP
Bolivia sends the first interim PRSP to the World Bank Board.

First Full PRSP
Uganda's update to its poverty plan is the first full PRSP submitted to the World Bank Board.

2001
Supporting PRSPs
A multidonor trust fund is set up to strengthen the preparation and implementation of national PRSPs in low-income countries.

Comprehensive Development Framework

Long-term Holistic Vision ⟷ **Country Ownership** ⟷ **Partnership** ⟷ **Development Results**

implementation, and poverty reduction strategies have survived transitions in national governments in several countries, while incorporating adaptations to reflect the programs of the incoming administrations.

PRSPs have put poverty reduction and the Millennium Development Goals at the center of the public policy debate in low-income countries, highlighting the need to identify and address country-specific constraints to more effective development. They have also heightened awareness of the need for sound analysis to underpin policy choices and reinforced incentives to monitor the results of public actions. In Vietnam, for example, the process of defining country-specific targets and indicators highlighted the importance of improving equity and the need to focus on regions and social groups not benefiting from growth.

PRSPs have also opened space for previously excluded stakeholders to engage in a national dialogue on economic policy and poverty reduction. The private sector is more active in consultations and, in some cases, through more formal mechanisms. Trade unions often were not present early on, but they have joined the dialogue in many countries. Governments have also attempted to broaden participation to include the voices of marginalized groups. In Cambodia the PRSP reflected the concerns of civil society organizations that there should be greater scrutiny of the impacts on poverty and society of key policies that affect the poor.

But implementation has varied across countries, and even within individual countries over time. The PRSP is an instrument charged with multiple objectives, many resulting in tradeoffs—between, say, long-term ambition and fiscal constraints, between comprehensiveness in addressing the different dimensions of poverty and focus, between meeting the expectations of

2002
Taking Stock
An international conference is held in Washington, D.C., on the PRSP approach, with representatives of governments, civil society organizations, and development partners.

2004
Broad Application
By the end of the year, 42 countries are implementing PRSPs.

the international community and ensuring country ownership and implementation capacity. These tradeoffs have been most difficult to resolve where PRSPs were developed independent of other planning processes and their role in government decision making was unclear. There are cases where finance ministries were not fully engaged in the process, undermining the link to the budget.

Participation in PRSP formulation has tended to be broad rather than deep, with a wide range of stakeholders engaged, but to only a limited extent. And civil society organizations have pointedly criticized some aspects of the participatory process. A persistent criticism from civil society organizations is that they are asked to react to existing programs rather than contribute to an overall rethinking of the government's program. Another complaint has been that some policies underpinning the PRSP, particularly the macroeconomic framework, are not sufficiently open to public debate. And after PRSPs are finalized and translated into action, it has not always been clear how participatory processes should endure.

Despite the shortcomings, the poverty reduction strategy approach is important for the World Bank's relations with low-income countries. It empowers governments to set their development priorities and pushes donors to align their assistance around a country's priorities rather than their own. It defines an operational framework for countries to specify the policies, programs, and resources needed to reduce poverty faster. And it provides a framework for mutual accountability by countries and donors, subject to continual learning and adaptation, as new insights are gained from implementation.

2005
A Second Generation
Several countries are working on their second full PRSP.

5

THE DECADE 1995–2005 SAW BOTH THE MATURING OF THE ENVIRONMENTALLY and Socially Sustainable Development network and the transformation of its business. The Bank journeyed from confrontation with NGOs to partnership. The environmental agenda moved from strengthening safeguards to embedding environment in development. Social development, a relatively new domain at the beginning of the decade, moved to the heart of development effectiveness.

We have a much richer understanding today of the many pathways by which environment and natural resource issues affect the welfare of poor countries and poor households within poor countries. The past 10 years have also seen a deepening and maturing of the social development agenda toward one that puts empowerment of people at the center of development.

Ensuring environmental and social responsibility

The Bank has a range of fiduciary responsibilities for its lending activities. In particular there are important questions concerning the potential environmental and social spillovers of Bank lending, and the steps that can be taken to prevent or mitigate these effects.

The World Bank was the first multilateral development institution to formally define a set of safeguard policies to enhance the environmental and social impacts of its lending. Built around the Operational Policy on Environmental Assessment, the 10 policies define required actions with respect to natural habitats, pest management, involuntary resettlement, indigenous peoples, forests, safety of dams, cultural property, projects on international waterways, and projects in disputed areas. In 2003 donors signed the Rome

1997
Protecting the Environment and Reducing Poverty
Wolfensohn's speech at the UN Earth Summit in New York urges revitalization of environmental goals to limit climate change, ozone depletion, and desertification and to promote clean water and biodiversity.

1998
Reducing Pollution
The World Bank and the International Finance Corporation launch the *Pollution Prevention and Abatement Handbook*, codifying good practice on reducing the pollution intensity of industrial production.

Declaration on Harmonization, which committed the development community to harmonizing aid processes, including safeguards, in order to reduce burdens on recipient countries.

The Bank published its first report on corporate social responsibility in 2004. *Focus on Sustainability* details the Bank's governance, goals, business products and processes, and management and monitoring. Corporate social responsibility requires more than publishing a report, however. The Bank is actively enhancing the sustainability focus of World Bank products and services by supporting clients on corporate social responsibility as well as reducing the impacts of our corporate facilities. To cite one example, World Bank facilities in Washington, D.C., will be carbon-neutral in 2005, through the purchase of "green" electricity and buying offsets from the BioCarbon Fund.

A new environment and social agenda

The Bank's work on social development and the environment underwent a major transformation during the decade, evolving from "do no harm" to fully embracing the poverty agenda. The new paradigm focuses on integrating the environment into development and promoting social sustainability by empowering people.

Integrating the environment into development

While the Bank had the Environmental Work Program in 1995, it did not have an explicit environment strategy. This gap was filled with the publication of *Making Sustainable Commitments: An Environment Strategy for the World Bank* in 2001. It has three main parts:

1999

Fuel for Thought

The World Bank strategy for the energy sector, published as *Fuel for Thought*, is adopted by the Board.

2000

Community-Driven Development

The World Bank launches an initiative to scale up community-driven development.

Protecting Biodiversity

The $150 million Critical Ecosystem Partnership Fund is launched as a joint initiative of Conservation International, the World Bank, and the Global Environment Facility to better safeguard the world's threatened biological hot spots in developing countries and to create realistic alternatives for poor people to relieve the growing pressures on the environment.

- Quality of life—environmental and natural resource interventions that improve the welfare of the poor by dealing with health, livelihoods, and vulnerability.
- Quality of growth—the policies and institutions that deal with the potentially negative spillovers from growth.
- Quality of the global commons—dealing with the threats to welfare that arise from global warming, loss of biodiversity, and deterioration of the oceans.

Fuel for Thought, the Bank's energy strategy adopted in 2000, explicitly targets a balance between providing the poor with access to energy and protecting the environment. Its main goals include:

- Facilitating access to cleaner, more efficient modern fuels.
- Protecting the environment and human health by reducing particulate emission, eliminating leaded gasoline, and reducing the sulfur content of liquid fuels.
- Promoting environmentally sound energy resource development.
- Decreasing the contribution of the energy sector to global warming, by promoting lower carbon and renewable energy sources.
- Developing capacity for environmental regulation, monitoring, and enforcement.

The adoption in 2002 of *Sustaining Forests: A Development Strategy* placed the Bank on a new trajectory in forested countries. The new strategy is built around four global targets: poverty reduction through community forest management and development of agroforestry, aimed at improving the lives of the 500 million poor who are dependent on forest and tree resources; supporting sustainable forest management aimed at bringing 200 million

2000

Return to High-Risk, High-Reward Projects

The Chad-Cameroon Petroleum Development and Pipeline Project is approved.

Quality and Sustainability

The Environmentally and Socially Sustainable Development Network establishes its Quality Assurance and Compliance Unit.

Prototype Carbon Fund

Recognizing that global warming will have the greatest impact on the World Bank's borrowing client countries, the Board approves the establishment of the Prototype Carbon Fund to mitigate climate change, promote sustainable development, demonstrate the possibilities of public-private partnerships, and offer a "learning-by-doing" opportunity to stakeholders.

hectares of forest under independently verified and certified sustainable forest management regimes; improving governance in the sector; and investing in protection and conservation.

Reaching the Rural Poor: A Renewed Strategy for Rural Development was adopted in 2003. Key elements of the strategy include the promotion of worldwide trade policy reform, boosting rural financial services, enhancing agricultural productivity, and supporting agricultural science and new technologies. Protecting the environment and the soil resource is another cornerstone, with an emphasis on reducing desertification and soil degradation, improving water management, protecting biodiversity, and incorporating climate change in rural development planning.

In 2004 the Bank adopted the recommendations in *Water Resources Sector Strategy: Strategic Directions for World Bank Engagement.* The key message is that the Bank will reengage with high-risk, high-reward hydraulic infrastructure, while aiming for high development impact, protecting the rights of those affected, implementing environmental and social safeguards, and ensuring timely decisions on project finance.

Revitalizing analytical work has been a key part of increasing the Bank's effectiveness on environmental issues. New products include the Country Environmental Analysis and Strategic Environmental Assessment. New research has begun to enrich our understanding of the links between poverty and the environment, including work on the health impacts of unsafe water, lack of sanitation, and dirty cooking fuels and on the welfare impacts of devolution of natural resource management.

Publication of environmental indicators and environmental accounts helps the Bank and its clients set priorities for environmental work. Beginning in

2001
First Environmental Strategy
The World Bank adopts its first comprehensive strategy for environment and development, *Making Sustainable Commitments.*

2002
Sharpening the Focus on Sustainable Development
The *World Development Report 2003: Sustainable Development in a Dynamic World* is launched, focusing on the growth in income and productivity required in developing countries to eliminate poverty in a way that is environmentally and socially sustainable.

The World Summit on Sustainable Development is held in Johannesburg, South Africa, to focus the world's attention on meeting the challenges of improving people's lives and conserving natural resources in a world that is growing in population.

The *Social Analysis Sourcebook* codifies good practice on incorporating social dimensions in investment projects.

1997, the *World Development Indicators* presented 60 environment and natural resource indicators for over 150 countries, including measures of "genuine" saving rates adjusted to reflect resource depletion.

Partnerships were also key to integrating environment and development. The Global Environment Facility (GEF) is the implementing mechanism for the global environmental conventions, and the World Bank, along with UNDP and the United Nations Environment Programme, is an implementing agency. From 1995 to the present the World Bank's cumulative GEF portfolio has grown from roughly $400 million to $1.7 billion. The major investments are in biodiversity conservation, climate change, and international waters.

The Critical Ecosystems Partnership Fund, established in 2000, aims to provide funding to preserve the most biologically significant and threatened areas of the world. It provides financial support, technical expertise, field knowledge, and information primarily to nongovernmental, community, and grassroots organizations in developing countries. By the end of fiscal 2004 it had provided support to 13 biodiversity hotspots and made grants totaling nearly $45 million to 189 civil society organizations.

The World Bank–World Wildlife Fund Alliance for Forest Conservation and Sustainable Use aims to achieve significantly reduced rate of loss and degradation of all forest types. The alliance's goals are aligned with the World Bank Forest Strategy—to establish 50 million hectares of new forest protected areas, to bring an equal area of existing forest reserves under effective management, and to bring 200 million hectares of the world's production forests under independently certified sustainable management.

2002

Sustaining Forests

The World Bank adopts a Forests Operational Policy and endorses *Sustaining Forests: A Development Strategy,* charting a path for the Bank's proactive engagement in forests, safeguarding the environmental values intrinsic to sustainability.

Reaching the Rural Poor

The Bank adopts a Rural Development Strategy to increase support for agriculture and rural development, with a specific focus on improving the lives of the rural poor.

BioCarbon Fund Launched

The World Bank launches an unprecedented opportunity for the poorest farmers and rural communities all over the developing world with the $100 million BioCarbon Fund, a public-private partnership that provides finance for reducing greenhouse gas emissions.

Promoting social sustainability by empowering people

People matter. This statement will be one of Jim Wolfensohn's most enduring legacies. Not only did Wolfensohn energize the Bank to focus on a "world free of poverty," he clearly advocated that if development is to achieve this, it must include social dimensions.

Wolfensohn passionately believed in empowering poor people—where people ceased to be merely the passive recipients of aid to active participants. He declared, "Poor people are not a liability but are assets..." He also believed that development must be comprehensive: "We should be addressing the question of poverty not just from economics, but because dealing with equity and social justice is right."

This belief in empowering people and looking beyond economic solutions to multidisciplinary approaches has ensured that social development is now seen as crucial in promoting human security, poverty reduction, and sustainable development. With the goal of empowering poor people, the World Bank is now recognized as making a valuable contribution toward transforming institutions for more inclusive, cohesive, and accountable societies.

Wolfensohn helped shift the global development dialogue toward recognizing the value of social development. He proposed the Comprehensive Development Framework, which was followed by the Poverty Reduction Strategy Papers (PRSPs)—an approach that embraced social development issues, such as the inclusion and empowerment of poor people through participatory approaches.

The past 10 years have thus seen a deepening and maturing of the social development agenda toward one that puts empowerment of people at the

2003
Water Strategy Approved
The World Bank Board approves the *Water Resources Sector Strategy.*

2004
Extractive Industries Review Reports
This consultative review presents a set of recommendations to guide involvement of the World Bank Group in the oil, gas, and mining sectors. The Bank commits to increasing renewable energy investments, strengthening consultation in affected communities, and improving transparency in the extractive sectors.

center of development. This process has involved evolution along several significant paths:

- *From the "do-no-harm" approach to social analysis to improving development outcomes.* This strategic shift in the Bank's approach is best illustrated through the work on indigenous peoples, which has evolved from protecting indigenous people to placing vulnerable groups at the center of development so that they can have control over their own future.
- *From protection to empowerment.* The *World Development Report 2000/2001: Attacking Poverty* draws attention to the multidimensional nature of poverty and identifies opportunity, empowerment, and security as three channels to reduce poverty.
- *A maturing partnership agenda.* The Bank has initiated civil society assessments of the enabling environment for civic engagement and social accountability at the country level. Analytical tools have been developed and piloted to feed into upstream analytical work, which seeks to deepen the understanding of opportunities and constraints to effective civic engagement.
- *From safety nets to scaling up community-driven development programs.* Backed by strong support from the Bank's president and senior managers, Bank lending for community-driven development increased from roughly $500 million in 1996 to $2.3 billion in fiscal 2001, a level sustained over the last three years.
- *From project to macro-level engagement.* Engagement at the macro-level became significant with the advent of PRSPs. There was widespread support among donors and civil society organizations for high quality, multistakeholder participation in PRSP processes and for poverty and

2005

Social Development Strategy

"Empowering People by Transforming Institutions: Social Development in World Bank Operations" identifies three operational principles—inclusion, cohesion, and accountability—as essential elements of equitable and sustainable development.

Using Country Systems

The Bank adopts an operational policy, Piloting the Use of Borrower Systems, to begin testing the use of a country's own environmental and social systems in Bank-financed operations, facilitating a move away from the application of the Bank's safeguard and fiduciary policies only to Bank-financed projects toward a focus on supporting the development and application of effective policies for all government spending.

social impact analysis of poverty reforms. The focus on ex ante analysis of the distributional impacts of proposed reforms provides the opportunity to increase the pro-poor impact of policy and institutional reforms.

The way forward

As the Kyoto Protocol enters in force, 2005 will be a key year for climate initiatives. Climate change poses severe risks to developing countries and to the development process itself, with effects on water resources, agriculture, forestry, fisheries, human settlements, ecological systems, and human health. For these countries, providing access to carbon finance and assistance with adaptation to climate change are essential steps toward sustainability.

Achieving the Millennium Development Goals will require growth, but not growth at any price. Responsible growth, which embraces social and environmental sustainability, is needed to maintain the increases in human welfare, in health, in skills, in social equity, and in the conservation of nature, that are the targets of the Goals.

At reasonable rates of population and output growth the world economy in 2050 will be four times what it is today. An economy this size poses enormous risks. An important part of the World Bank's role going forward must be helping poor countries to manage these risks: new technology, new infrastructure, new sources of energy, new models of resource management, new financial mechanisms for global public goods—all areas where the Bank and its development partners can make a difference. The vision of a more equitable world in 2050 will depend critically on achieving inclusion, cohesion, and accountability.

2005

A "Greener" World Bank

The World Bank headquarters facilities become carbon-neutral.

6

AS THE COLD WAR WOUND DOWN AND INTERNAL CONFLICTS BECAME MORE prevalent in the early 1990s, no one in the UN system or in NGOs working in the relief and rehabilitation programs of Liberia, Kurdistan, or the former Yugoslavia could be heard to ask, "Where is the Bank?" As the premier development agency, better known for the controversy over structural adjustment, its absence was taken for granted. Yet by the time East Timor's struggle for independence burst onto the world scene, a Bank team was in the vanguard of the rehabilitation and reconstruction wave. Today, the Bank is fully engaged in a wide range of conflict-affected countries and a number of fragile states, which are often beset by conflict or have never recovered from its aftereffects.

Putting the "R" back in the International Bank for Reconstruction and Development (IBRD) has been a case study in institutional change and adaptation, as the Bank has sought to respond to a more complex international environment and to reconcile a sensitivity to conflict with its poverty reduction mission.

The Bank's early involvement in postconflict reconstruction focused on providing financial capital and rebuilding physical infrastructure—picking up the pieces after the guns fell silent. But in a post–Cold War era marked by an increase in the number and severity of civil conflicts, the Bank found that it had to adapt to different and more complex challenges. Two events in the mid-1990s prompted a turning point in its approach to conflict. The first came in 1994 when the Bank was asked to administer the multidonor Holst Fund for the West Bank and Gaza. The second came in 1995 when the Bank was asked to take the lead with the European Commission in planning and coordinating international postconflict assistance for Bosnia and

1995
Rebuilding Bosnia
The Bank is asked to take the lead with the European Commission in planning and coordinating postconflict assistance to Bosnia and Herzegovina, with Bank financing alone resulting in 14 projects being approved the following year.

Herzegovina. The Bosnia program in particular broke the mold and formed the basis for a new postconflict approach.

Realizing that it faced a far more difficult postconflict environment and growing expectations in the international community, the Bank decided to create a locus of expertise in postconflict reconstruction and to examine its rules of engagement. In 1997 the Bank created the Post-Conflict Unit in the Social Development Department, and the Executive Directors endorsed *A Framework for World Bank Involvement in Post-Conflict Reconstruction*, which set out the rationale and guidelines for Bank involvement in countries transitioning from conflict, but the focus remained firmly on postconflict reconstruction.

The small Post-Conflict Unit located in the center, comprising mainly former UN and NGO staff, set about adding teeth to the new postconflict framework. But the real changes became apparent in the Bank's regions. Funding, analysis, and expertise started moving away from a narrow focus on reconstruction, flowing instead toward new areas—demobilization and reintegration, child soldiers, land-mine clearance, community-based rehabilitation, and state building. As one NGO commentator drily put it, "So the Bank has discovered peace." What the Bank had really discovered was that in practice postconflict was where we all wanted to get to, but was not always the starting point.

As the Bank's postconflict agenda took hold, and with the costs, complexity, risks, and visibility of reconstruction operations running so high, attention then turned to prevention. Here, research added a new impetus to the Bank's agenda. In 1999 the Bank's research arm under Paul Collier opened the global debate on the economic causes and consequences of conflict. For an institution well stocked with economists, there had been surprisingly scant Bank economic analysis or explanations of conflict. Bank

1997

Strengthening Support for Postconflict Recovery

Management presents to the World Bank Board a policy paper, *A Framework for World Bank Involvement in Postconflict Reconstruction*, aimed at strengthening support for postconflict recovery, taking the institution back to its original mandate (the Bank's first loan was for reconstruction of war-ravaged France in 1947).

Post-Conflict Fund and Post-Conflict Unit Established

The World Bank establishes the Post-Conflict Fund to enhance its ability to support countries in transition from conflict to sustainable peace and economic growth, as well as establishing its own Post-Conflict Unit.

economists tended to think of conflict as an exogenous shock, akin to a natural disaster or an adverse swing in the terms of trade—something bad and unfortunate that happened occasionally but either was "not our problem" or in any case "there was not much we could do about it."

With poverty both a cause and a consequence of conflict, and in line with evolving international initiatives to explore the potential role of development assistance in preventing conflict, toward the late 1990s the Bank sought to redefine its reconstruction role more broadly—from an approach focused on reconstruction to one that seeks to understand the root causes of conflict and to integrate a sensitivity to conflict in Bank activities. In line with this shift in focus, and following discussions inside and outside the institution, the Board in January 2001 approved a new operational policy, Development Cooperation and Conflict, defining the Bank's approach to conflict-affected, not just postconflict, countries. The policy recognizes that the Bank can play a more proactive role in conflict-affected and vulnerable countries, and calls for Bank assistance to minimize potential causes and be sensitive to conflict.

The new policy set out three levels of Bank engagement in conflict-affected countries:

- A Watching Brief, where normal assistance is not possible because of conflict.
- A Transitional Support phase, where the Bank is reengaging but conditions are not yet appropriate for a full-fledged country assistance strategy.
- A normal phase, when the country successfully transitions out of conflict and the Bank can develop a country assistance strategy.

To signal this shift in emphasis, the Post-Conflict Unit was renamed the Conflict Prevention and Reconstruction Unit and, together with the Bank's

1999

IDA Focus on Postconflict Countries

IDA12 pilots new allocation procedures, subsequently formally adopted under IDA13 and confirmed in IDA14, which increase the IDA allocation for postconflict countries.

2001

Focus on Prevention

The World Bank Board adopts a new operational policy, Development Cooperation and Conflict, broadening the Bank's approach beyond postconflict to be more proactive in conflict-affected countries. The Bank's Post-Conflict Unit is renamed Conflict Prevention and Reconstruction Unit.

regions and networks, set about the task of translating the reality of "no development without peace" into analysis, tools, and operational guidance for Bank assistance and partnerships.

As the Bank widened its involvement in conflict, it also became clear that it had to take another look at its financing modalities. Three important innovations followed. First was the creation of a Post-Conflict Fund (PCF) in August 1997 to support countries transitioning out of conflict with grants implemented through UN, NGO, and client governments. As with the Bank's evolving approach to conflict, the PCF evolved and adapted to new demands by broadening the range of grants it can fund in line with the mandate under the new operational policy. PCF grant approvals since inception total close to $70 million over 140 projects across 37 countries and territories.

A second approach, and building on the Holst Fund, has been the use of multidonor trust funds to mobilize resources and increase funding flexibility in complex postconflict reconstruction programs. Multidonor trust funds can be flexibly adapted to cover areas where the Bank does not have expertise and where it needs to work in partnership with UN agencies and other donors, while ensuring support is channeled though a unified budgetary framework.

Third, in 2004 the Bank created a $25 million Low-Income Countries Under Stress (LICUS) Trust Fund (fiscal 2004–06) to support countries in nonaccrual status where IDA financing is unavailable and PCF funds are insufficient to finance more comprehensive LICUS strategies.

The Bank and its partners also focused on ways to make IDA more flexible and better able to provide more concessional funding to countries with high postconflict needs. IDA12 piloted a new allocation procedure for postconflict

2001

Failed States a Threat

Terrorist attacks show that failed states offer fertile ground for terrorism to thrive.

THE LOW-INCOME COUNTRIES UNDER STRESS INITIATIVE

The Low-Income Countries Under Stress (LICUS) Initiative is the World Bank's response to the need for improving development aid effectiveness in fragile states. It covers countries at the bottom of the Country Policy and Institutional Assessment rating system—25 countries in 2005. They may be postconflict or conflict-vulnerable countries, countries with weak or dysfunctional institutions, or strong regimes with a particularly poor governance record.

Fragile states are home to more than 500 million of the world's most disadvantaged citizens. In addition to locking their own population in poverty, they provide fertile ground for cross-border spillovers of conflict, economic instability, organized crime, terrorism, refugee flows, and epidemic diseases. The donor community has in the past few years paid more attention to the problems of these most marginalized countries. We all realize that aid is used more effectively in countries with stronger policies, but it is important not to leave behind the weaker countries.

The World Bank's LICUS Unit was established at the end of 2002 to help coordinate the Bankwide LICUS Initiative. The new unit is a departure for the Bank—in two senses. It is located at the heart of operational policy division, directly linking regions and country departments, senior management, and the institutional departments that are responsible for setting rules and mobilizing human and financial resources. The country grouping recognizes that all fragile states require close management attention, whether they are facing declining governance, prolonged political crisis or conflict, postconflict transition, or a gradual movement toward reform.

The initiative has focused on three main areas in the past two years.

- First, it has worked to support country departments in better adapting their strategies to country context. In the eight countries where the Bank had completely disengaged, it has rebuilt the analytical base and knowledge of institutional players. This has been critical to positioning the Bank to reengage quickly when needed, as was the case in Liberia, Sudan, and Haiti. Together with the UN Development Group, the Bank has piloted a new planning tool—the transitional results framework—to integrate political, security, economic, and social actions in one unified plan and budget.
- Second, it has coordinated institutional reforms to improve the Bank's response in fragile states. This has included increasing budgets for analytical work, changing the performance measurement system, amending the IDA framework to take account of failed states that do not meet the full postconflict criteria, improving human resource incentives, and creating the LICUS trust fund to finance small-scale engagement in countries that are in nonaccrual to the Bank.
- Third, it is responsible for external work with other development partners. In January 2005, the Bank sponsored a process with the Organisation for Economic Co-operation and Development/Development Assistance Committee, the UN, and the European Commission to consider how to improve development effectiveness in fragile states. This resulted in agreement by OECD members on a set of Principles for International Engagement in Fragile States. Aiming to improve coherence among the interventions of development, diplomatic, and defense actors in these countries, the principles stress the need for unified planning, fast and flexible action, and long-term commitment.

—Sarah F. Cliffe

countries, formally adopted under IDA13 and confirmed under IDA14. For a limited period it provides higher allocations than a country would receive under the normal performance-based criteria (four years of higher allocations and three years of transition to normal allocations), and defines a set of performance indicators specifically tailored to postconflict conditions. Under IDA13 postconflict countries also could receive up to 40 percent as grants, and in special cases territories under UN administration could be eligible for IDA grants. The new framework allowed IDA to greatly expand its support to postconflict countries—the Board approved credits to 11 eligible countries/territories totaling $3.2 billion under IDA13, compared to only 5 countries and $815 million under IDA12. Of total commitments under IDA13, $1 billion was in the form of 29 postconflict grants. The IDA12 framework also recognized the problem of arrears in postconflict countries, authorizing as a last resort the use of small grant funding to postconflict countries with large and protracted arrears.

September 11 also prompted the Bank to look anew at its mission and mandate. The proximity of the attacks had a palpable effect on Bank staff and led to a genuine soul-searching and reexamination of the core Bank mission. Wolfensohn was quick to articulate what most staff felt—that the poverty reduction mission was more important than ever. It wasn't that poverty led to terrorism—the poor are not the enemy—but a sense that "failed states" offered fertile grounds for terrorism to thrive. Although small-scale terrorists can lurk in the shadows of any society, September 11 showed that large-scale terrorism needs territory outside the control of a recognized and reputable government.

2002
LICUS Initiative Launched
The Low-Income Countries Under Stress Initiative is established to address the special challenges facing countries with very weak policies and institutions.

2004
LICUS Trust Fund Established
The Trust Fund supports LICUS with the most severe conflict and institutional problems in implementing the reforms necessary for reengaging the international community.

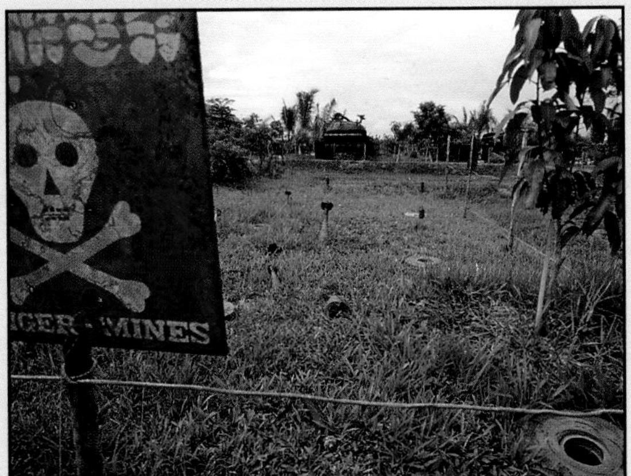

September 11 also roughly coincided with another important round of research and policy debate, which became known as the "aid effectiveness" debate. The research findings implied that donors should be more selective in allocating aid, rewarding the good performers, and, in the extreme, cutting off bad performers—a tough-love approach. Although the case for performance-based aid was persuasive, there was a sense of unease about setting the poor performers adrift. More than 500 million people live in these countries and, through no fault of their own, suffer the consequences of incompetent or failed states. September 11 added a new dimension by painfully showing that the problems of poor performers would not be contained within their borders. The Bank's response was to reexamine its role in countries with weak policies and institutions—which it labeled LICUS—more than three-quarters of them affected by conflict.

Two important challenges will figure prominently as the Bank continues to adapt its approach. First, the Bank will need to define its role within the proposed reforms to the UN system and a growing international consensus on the need for a more comprehensive approach to human security. Second, it is neither rhetoric nor exaggeration to say that the conflict and development agenda has been mainstreamed in Bank operations, but it has made far less progress in addressing conflicts that have a regional dimension. It has made an important start with the Multidonor Trust Fund for Demobilization and Reintegration for Africa's Great Lakes region, but it continues to struggle to adopt regional approaches in other settings such as West Africa and the Horn of Africa.

The Mostar Bridge Rises Again

An example of the Bank's intensified engagement in postconflict reconstruction is the restoration of Bosnia-Herzegovina's Mostar Bridge. After surviving the two world wars that ravaged the region, it was destroyed by civil war in 1993. Built in 1566, this stunning architectural achievement had been one of the country's greatest cultural treasures and a symbol of people connecting with each other. The World Bank financed one-third of the $12 million reconstruction costs.

7

WHEN JIM WOLFENSOHN BECAME PRESIDENT OF THE BANK IN JUNE 1995, DEBT relief, like the "c" word (corruption), was barely mentioned in the corridors. Unpopular among leaders in rich countries, barring some notable exceptions, debt relief was considered well-nigh impossible. But Wolfensohn felt otherwise, with a conviction that combined his passion for development with his understanding of finance. He encouraged the staff to prepare a proposal on the issue.

When the proposal was first revealed, it met strong resistance from some creditors, but ultimately gained acceptance with the launch in 1996 of the Heavily Indebted Poor Countries (HIPC) Initiative—an official joint Bank-Fund program to oversee debt relief to the world's poorest countries. Wolfensohn's participation—and the World Bank's involvement—in the global debate on debt relief for the poorest and most heavily indebted countries was influenced in no small measure by activist NGOs—initially Oxfam International, and later the Jubilee movement—which raised international awareness on the issue and put considerable pressure on the leaders of rich countries and the international financial institutions.

The business case

In advocating debt relief, Wolfensohn brought together his recognition of the business imperatives and his deeply held belief that debt relief was also a moral question. The business case begins with the recognition that high levels of debt are an impediment to growth and poverty reduction—a key objective of development. Heavy debt burdens tend to dampen private investment, focus government efforts on short-term policies, and divert scarce funds from priority projects. Low growth and high debt tend to

1995
Change of Direction
In his Annual Meetings address, Wolfensohn indicates a need for the World Bank to consider debt relief.

reinforce each other, forming a deadly debt trap that can retard development for decades. Wolfensohn advocates debt relief because it is the only sensible business decision in such circumstances. But he emphasizes that debt relief must be accompanied by increased development assistance, because "financing debt relief by cutting development assistance would be a cruel hoax on the poor."

The moral case

Wolfensohn believes that economics and spirituality are inseparable and fundamental to human dignity. This was reflected in a commentary in the *Globe and Mail* (June 1999), in which Wolfensohn and George Carey, the Archbishop of Canterbury, wrote: "It is perhaps important to establish at the outset that we both firmly believe that debt, when it contributes to poverty, is a moral issue. No poor country should ever lack the resources to educate its children or treat its sick because of debt. But our morality—indeed, our humanity—is tested not only by our solutions to daunting problems, but by the commitment and good will we bring to solving them."

Contributions to the main principles of debt relief

At various times in his campaign to make debt relief an accepted instrument of development finance for the poorest countries, Jim Wolfensohn crafted the key principles that have now become enshrined in the continuing global debate on debt relief and codified in the HIPC Initiative.

- *Debt relief must be additional to development assistance.* According to Wolfensohn, debt relief "must complement, not replace, development assistance. Poverty is related to many factors: crumbling schools,

1996
Commitment to Debt Relief
The World Bank pledges $500 million to a special trust fund for debt relief of heavily indebted poor countries (HIPC).

1997
First HIPC Beneficiary
Uganda begins to receive debt relief as the first country to reach its decision point under the HIPC Initiative. Upon reaching the completion point a year later, Uganda qualifies for $650 million in total relief.

overstretched health care, impassable roads, polluted air and water, poor governance, lack of investment, and, sometimes, severe indebtedness. We must address all these causes within a comprehensive development strategy that combines debt reduction and aid."

- *Debt relief must be an integral part of a broader development architecture.* Wolfensohn has stressed that debt relief is not a panacea for development and must be accompanied by strong policy reforms. "While debt relief is critically important, it will help reduce poverty only if developing countries continue the hard work of improving economic management. There is much to discuss about which policies best support poverty reduction. But there is no argument that runaway deficits and inflation punish the poor most; subsidies that benefit elites are unfair; and corruption strangles the weakest first." It is for this reason that the HIPC Initiative countries are asked to implement programs under the IMF's Poverty Reduction and Growth Facility (PRGF), implement poverty reduction strategies for at least a year, and implement structural reforms agreed with the World Bank that cover such diverse areas as public expenditure management, anticorruption actions, and state-enterprise reforms.
- *Debt relief must be aligned with other policies and actions of the international community.* Jim Wolfensohn has reminded the international community that its responsibility does not stop with debt relief. "The combination of improved policies and debt relief will not be enough in most cases. We need to make sure that the HIPC Initiative is supported by all creditors, including official bilateral and commercial creditors that have yet to provide the required debt relief. More broadly, we call upon

1999

Debt Relief for Six Countries

Since the launching of the HIPC Initiative (1996–99) debt relief totaling about $3 billion has been agreed for six countries—Bolivia, Burkina Faso, Guyana, Mali, Mozambique, and Uganda.

Enhanced HIPC Initiative

The initiative is enhanced to provide deeper, broader, and faster debt relief to participating countries. The links between debt relief and poverty reduction are strengthened so that resources freed by debt relief will be used to promote growth and help reduce poverty.

industrial countries to raise their official development assistance toward internationally agreed levels. And we urge them to open their markets to the exports of the poor countries, giving them a better chance to succeed on their own."

- *Debt relief should be used for poverty reduction.* Wolfensohn has made it clear that debt relief should have a direct beneficial impact on poor people. "New resources will enable governments to sharply increase desperately needed social investments; following debt relief, social expenditures are rising to between two and three times debt service obligations. As a result, millions more children will have a chance to learn to read and write; health clinics and rural roads and sanitation facilities will be built; AIDS programs will reach out to the afflicted. And already, people, working with their governments, are charting their own development course."
- *Debt relief should not jeopardize the financial integrity of the international financial institutions.* Wolfensohn countered efforts to make the international financial institutions deliver debt relief without infusions of new finance. "It's a great idea to forgive debt, but if you do, let's make sure that the amount you forgive is matched by new funds, otherwise you won't be able to lend in the future."
- *Debt relief must be accompanied by additional efforts to ensure long-term debt sustainability.* Wolfensohn believes that debt relief can help with debt sustainability but cannot guarantee it. For that, additional action is needed. "Access to external capital is fundamental to any country's development, but borrowers and lenders need to be vigilant about the long-term sustainability of the resulting debt. In many instances this

2000

Global Focus on Debt Relief

International focus on HIPC debt grows with the Jubilee 2000 Debt Relief Rally in Washington.

Implementation

The modifications introduced by the enhanced HIPC Initiative made additional countries eligible. With continued pressure by civil society and the impatience of the Development Committee at the seemingly slow pace of progress, implementation is accelerated: 22 countries reach their decision points by the end of 2000.

will mean shifting to grants, and strictly limiting new lending to only the most generous terms."

Ten years ago, debt relief was not on the World Bank's agenda. Nor was it considered a priority by the international community more widely. Today, largely thanks to Wolfensohn's drive for an initiative for the heavily indebted poor countries, 27 countries are receiving debt relief on the order of $54 billion, and many more are expected to benefit. The debt of these countries has been slashed by two-thirds, and their debt-service ratios reduced by one-third to one-half. There is now considerable evidence that the savings from debt relief are being used for poverty programs integral to country-designed poverty reduction strategies. The Bank and Fund are about to launch a joint framework for debt sustainability in low-income countries. And the global debate on additional debt relief to help finance the Millennium Development Goals acknowledges the principles of debt relief that have been widely accepted as a result of Wolfensohn's leadership.

Challenges going forward

Despite much progress on debt relief under the HIPC Initiative and through additional voluntary debt relief by important bilateral official creditors, high debt burdens remain a challenge to future development progress in many poor countries. The new debt sustainability framework remains untested, and even if it is successful, it will help reduce debt burdens only over many years. In the meantime, poor countries need additional resources to progress toward the MDGs and remain vulnerable to external shocks from natural disasters and sharp downturns in their terms of trade. In responding to these challenges, the international community has embarked on many initiatives:

2001
Development Committee Communiqué
With the Development Committee Communiqué from the 64th meeting, held in Ottawa, Canada, ministers welcome the continuing progress in implementing the HIPC Initiative and reiterate their commitment to the enhanced HIPC Initiative as a means of achieving a lasting exit from unsustainable debt for eligible countries.

2002
Beijing Speech
In a speech at Peking University, Wolfensohn notes: "We have learned that debt reduction for the most highly indebted poor countries is a crucial element in putting countries back on their feet, and that the funds released can be used effectively for poverty programs."

- *Delivering additional debt relief by the Bretton Woods Institutions and regional development banks* while maintaining their financial integrity and protecting their role as a principal source of long-term development finance and policy advice to the poorest countries of the world. Prominent among these actions is the UK government's proposal to provide its share of 100 percent debt relief on debt service payments owed by selected poor countries until 2015.
- *Providing a higher level of grants in support of poverty reduction strategies* so that the external financing the poorest countries need to meet the MDGs does not come at the expense of future debt sustainability in the poorest countries.
- *Building an international architecture for helping developing countries deal with exogenous shocks,* so that development programs and progress toward the MDGs do not stall in the event of natural disasters or sharp downward movements in the terms of trade.
- *Continuing the implementation of the HIPC Initiative,* especially bringing to the decision point HIPC Initiative countries that are not yet receiving debt relief—a difficult task, since most of these countries are affected by conflict, have weak governance structures, and suffer from intractable arrears problems.

2004
Extension of the Sunset Clause
The sunset clause is extended by another two years, through 2006, to provide the opportunity for the remaining HIPC Initiative countries to qualify for relief.

2005
Expanding Relief
HIPC debt relief totaling $54 billion reaches 27 countries, with those countries' external debt reduced by one-half on average and by two-thirds when combined with existing debt-relief programs.

8

IN THE EARLY 1990S THE BANK EXPLICITLY RECOGNIZED THAT THE PROCESSES and the institutions by which authority in a country is exercised are key factors for development. Governance, to put it in Bank terminology, had been found to foster strong and equitable development as long as it is not only efficient, effective, transparent, and free of corruption, but also and most of all, inclusive. As a consequence, the Bank began working on good governance and identified the rule of law as a key element of this new concept. It is courts, after all, that hold governments accountable. It is courts of law that give those seeking justice a forum to exercise their rights, including rights vis-à-vis the State. And are policies not embedded in laws? Legal and judicial reforms thus were identified as the means of promoting the rule of law.

But when Jim Wolfensohn assumed the leadership of the World Bank in 1995, legal and judicial reform was a relative newcomer to the development agenda. He made legal and judicial reform a key element of his Comprehensive Development Framework and a tool in the effort to control corruption. His presidency raised awareness of the role of rule of law in economic growth and equitable development.

The initial momentum and demand for legal and judicial reform in client countries had been created by the end of the Cold War and the transition toward more market-oriented economies and open societies. Jim Wolfensohn knew how to use this momentum for the broader development agenda. He labored to ensure that the focus on this transition process did not leave out the poor, especially in Africa. Under his presidency, nearly 20 percent of legal and judicial reform activities funded by the Bank were carried out in Europe and Central Asia, but Africa still came first with an impressive 25 percent of all legal and judicial reform activities.

1996
Cancer of Corruption
In a break with the Bank's historical practice of avoiding the topic as political, Wolfensohn addresses corruption as an obstacle to development in his Annual Meetings address, buttressing the Bank's work on legal and judicial reform.

1999
Legal Reform in the CDF
The Bank launches the Comprehensive Development Framework, with legal and judicial reform as one of its four main pillars.

Jim Wolfensohn also made it clear that legal and judicial reforms are not objectives by themselves, but instruments to achieve development goals. As early as 1996 he identified the "cancer of corruption" as a major impediment to development, breaking a taboo that had seriously hindered the effectiveness and credibility of the World Bank's work to fight poverty. It became clear to him that the fight against corruption cannot be successful without anticorruption laws and a well-functioning justice system that is able to enforce them.

He then recognized legal and judicial reform as one of the four structural pillars of the Comprehensive Development Framework, presented in 1999. This decisive step moved legal and judicial reform into the mainstream of the international development agenda. As he would put it some years later in a keynote address at the Woodrow Wilson Center, "We have learned that any effort to fight poverty must be comprehensive. There is no magic bullet that alone will slay poverty, but we know too that there are conditions that foster successful development: education and health programs to build the human capacity of the country, good and clean government, an effective legal and justice system, and a well-organized and supervised financial system."

Under Jim Wolfensohn's presidency, the World Bank, in partnership with others, organized a series of global and regional conferences on the rule of law and development, bringing together judges, parliamentarians, senior government officials, partner donor agencies, legal experts, economists, political and social scientists, scholars and experts in the field, development specialists, court administrators, civil society representatives, and Bank staff. The cycle started in 2000 with the Global Conference on Comprehensive Legal

Unless you have equity, unless you have justice, unless you address the issues of poverty, there can be no peace. And without legal and judicial reform, in my judgment, there can be no peace.

James D. Wolfensohn
Washington, D.C.
June 5–7, 2000

2000
Global Attention to Legal and Judicial Reform
The Bank is lead organizer for the first Global Conference on Comprehensive Legal and Judicial Development, in Washington, D.C.

and Judicial Development in Washington, D.C., and continued with the St. Petersburg conference in 2001 on Empowerment, Opportunity, and Security through Law and Justice, the Marrakech conference in 2002 on Strategies for Modernizing the Judicial Sector in the Arab Countries, and the All-Africa Conference on Law, Justice, and Development in 2003 in Abuja, Nigeria.

These developments have had an important impact on the World Bank's portfolio in the field of legal and judicial reform. The number of Bank-funded legal and judicial reform activities has expanded to 16 active stand-alone projects in 2005, with another 7 projects in the pipeline. More than 25 legal and judicial sector assessments—prerequisites for identifying the challenges and designing appropriate project components—have been completed. In the past five years in Africa alone, 8 countries have had Bank-financed investment projects with judicial reform components, and 16 others have had grants providing support for judicial reform. In Latin America and the Caribbean the Bank has extended 10 investment loans in support of judicial reform over the same period. An adjustment operation in Argentina supported measures to modernize provincial courts. Seven countries in Latin America have benefited from grants. Assessments were carried out in Argentina and Ecuador, and other research and analytical work was conducted in eight countries, as well as two regional studies and two conferences.

The types of legal and judicial reforms supported by the Bank reflect the many challenges facing judiciaries in developing and transition countries. Interventions to build judicial capacity include development of comprehensive judicial reform strategies and action plans, modernization and automation

2001

Opportunity through the Rule of Law

Building on the previous year's conference in Washington, D.C., the momentum continues with the St. Petersburg conference on Empowerment, Opportunity, and Security through Law and Justice.

of court administration and case management, improvement of court registries, construction and upgrading of court infrastructure, purchase of computers and information technologies, support to improve enforcement of judgments, training of judges and court professionals, and monitoring of judicial performance.

Bank projects to improve access to justice have supported the simplification of judicial procedures, the dissemination of legal information to lawyers and lay people, the provision of legal services to poor and vulnerable people, projects to improve delivery of legal services to women and minority groups, and support for alternative dispute resolution mechanisms (ADRs). On the country level, Bank projects support ADRs as a means of expanding access for the poor, as an efficient way of resolving commercial disputes, and as an adjunct to case management. On the international level, the Bank supports ADRs through the work of the International Centre for Settlement of Investment Disputes, a World Bank Group organization that applies conciliation and arbitration to resolve disputes between governments and foreign investors. Its caseload grew dramatically in the last decade, increasing from 5 cases and an amount in dispute of $15 million in 1995, to 85 cases and a total amount in dispute of more than $20 billion in 2005.

Development policy lending has been tied to anticorruption measures for the judiciary, judicial standards of service, criteria for selection of judicial staff, and measures to protect the independence of the judiciary, including rules on the appointment, disciplining, and career development of judges.

The Bank's continuing commitment to legal and judicial reform reflects the recognition that ineffective legal frameworks and institutions remain a critical impediment to poverty alleviation, both in their negative impact on

2005
ICSID
From handling 5 cases for an amount in dispute of $15 million in 1995, the International Centre for Settlement and Investment Disputes' caseload increases to 85 cases with a total amount in dispute of more than $20 billion.

the investment climate and their tendency to reinforce the exclusion of the poor and marginalized from participation in development. Corruption and elite capture within judicial systems are among the obstacles to development to overcome through legal and judicial reform. As the Bank works to help countries deliver justice services more effectively and more fairly, areas of the law such as criminal justice, human rights, and the role of traditional justice systems may require new responses from the Bank.

Jim Wolfensohn's promotion of legal and judicial reform within the broader development agenda has enabled the Bank to gain substantive knowledge about legal and judicial reform, and about the links among economic growth, equitable development, and the rule of law. Law and justice issues are now mainstreamed in the Bank's work, from gender and empowerment to civil service and finance. They are dealt with in a number of *World Development Reports,* and they are one of the criteria in Country Policy and Institutional Assessments. Wolfensohn raised awareness within the Bank and among our borrowers that the rule of law is necessary both for economic growth and equitable development. As he put it at the Global Forum on Fighting Corruption in 1999, "We cannot have a fight against continuing poverty, we cannot have equitable growth, indeed, I would suggest in the end we cannot have a peaceful world, if we do not address the issues of governance, corruption, and a legal and justice system that works."

As Wolfensohn's term comes to an end, the Bank has launched the Legal Modernization Initiative, bringing together many vice presidencies in a multidisciplinary approach to the field of legal and judicial reform. The Initiative focuses the Bank's in-depth analytical work and coordinates its

2005

Snapshot of Bank Work

The number of Bank-funded legal and judicial reform activities expands to 16 active standalone projects, augmented by components in many others, with 7 more such projects in the pipeline.

ability to assimilate global experience and expertise to respond to country-specific needs and circumstances, with the goal of helping countries deliver justice services more effectively and more fairly. Providing access to justice and legal education is a critical element in the Bank's work to empower poor people to participate in development. Supporting effective enforcement of laws is a key to Bank work to improve the investment climate. And strengthening judicial independence and accountability is essential in the fight against corruption.

2005
Legal Modernization Initiative
The Bank launches the Legal Modernization Initiative to strengthen its ability to help countries deliver justice more fairly.

9

CONTRARY TO POPULAR NOTIONS, THE CHALLENGE OF CORRUPTION IN development had not been absent from the Bank throughout its existence. But it was never embraced by the top leadership or shareholders and was thus not tackled explicitly as a core mandate in development. Often it was the determination and courage of a few staff writing about it that kept a small flame alive. The corruption challenge for the Bank had also evolved significantly between the 1950s and mid-1990s, mirroring the Bank's ideological swings as development strategies shifted, and because of its major scaling up in lending and its increased understanding thanks to the "power of data."

The evolution of the corruption challenge from a Bank historical perspective suggests that Jim Wolfensohn was the right person in the right place at the right time. This requires an understanding of the institution and of the times prior to Wolfensohn's arrival at the Bank. Such broader perspective, as well as the analysis of current achievements and challenges ahead in addressing corruption, is the subject of the paper "Corruption Matters at the Bank" (www.worldbank.org/wbi/governance), which includes a detailed chronology of historical milestones. The brief account here excerpts some descriptions of the various anticorruption components of the Bank's strategy during the Wolfensohn years. Nonetheless, it aims at giving a sense of the sea change in anticorruption during this period.

Arriving at the Bank in mid-1995, Wolfensohn already knew that corruption is an impediment to development. He knew that bribery and corruption could be found in the implementation of investment projects in many countries. And he knew that there was no reason to expect that Bank-funded projects would be immune to corruption risks in those countries.

1996

Cancer of Corruption

Wolfensohn identifies corruption as an obstacle to development in his Annual Meetings address.

1997

Anti-Corruption Strategy

The World Bank Board approves the Anti-Corruption Strategy, as spelled out in "Helping Countries Combat Corruption: The Role of the World Bank."

Internal Investigations

The Bank's Internal Auditing Department establishes a small investigations unit to pursue allegations of fraud and corruption.

Role of the State Report

The *World Development Report 1997: The State in a Changing World* examines what constitutes an effective state, including rules and institutions. It also analyzes corruption.

His October 1996 Annual Meetings address on the "Cancer of Corruption" was the first time the head of an international financial institution had ventured into this politically sensitive issue. It was meant to be more than signaling to the world that corruption was an important issue for development and poverty alleviation: he also shattered the taboo of addressing corruption, and provided a clear message that he intended to implement changes within the institution.

The address resonated with many constituencies in rich and poor countries. Shortly thereafter, in meetings with ministers of finance from countries in OECD and emerging economies, many were bringing up the challenge of corruption and making the case that more was needed to address it. Some were picking up the message from their various constituencies at home.

By the time of the 1997 Annual Meetings, the Bank had assembled a group of experts from various units that had prepared a strategy to address corruption, which was approved by the Board, capping an intensive effort spearheaded by Wolfensohn for well over a year. The strategy, spelled out in the report "Helping Countries Combat Corruption: The Role of the World Bank," laid out actions in four areas:

- Preventing fraud and corruption among staff and in its projects.
- Assisting countries in curbing corruption.
- Mainstreaming anticorruption into country analysis and lending.
- Partnering in international efforts to fight corruption.

Feeding the four pillars was "the power of data"—developing a major databank and diagnostics tool on governance and corruption.

We also need to address transparency, accountability, and institutional capacity. And let's not mince words: we need to deal with the cancer of corruption. In country after country, it is the people who are demanding action on this issue. They know that corruption diverts resources from the poor to the rich, increases the cost of running businesses, distorts public expenditures, and deters foreign investors.

James D. Wolfensohn
Annual Meetings address
October 1, 1996

1998

Strengthening Oversight

The Bank establishes its Oversight Committee on Fraud and Corruption to address possible instances of fraud and corruption among its staff.

Hotline Established

The World Bank sets up a hotline to receive anonymous reports of possible cases of fraud or corruption involving World Bank projects.

Addressing fraud and corruption in Bank-supported projects

To strengthen its financial control capacity, the Bank in 1997 adopted an improved framework on internal financial controls, now used widely by leading financial institutions. It has since helped clients strengthen their own capacities on financial management and procurement, and it supervises contracts through special audits. In 1998 the Oversight Committee on Fraud and Corruption was created to investigate allegations of corruption involving Bank staff and thereafter Bank-financed contracts as well. A 24-hour international hotline was also established.

A significant scaling up in institutionalizing the Bank's investigative arm for fraud and corruption took place in 2001 with the creation of the Department of Institutional Integrity, broadening the role in investigating claims of corruption, complemented by the Sanctions Committee to adjudicate cases and assess penalties to firms engaged in fraud and corruption. More than 300 companies and individuals have been barred from doing business with the Bank. The names of firms delisted from bidding on Bank-funded projects are publicly posted on the Bank's external Web site.

Helping countries that ask for assistance

By the late 1990s the Bank was implementing a strategy of anticorruption focused on a public sector management approach, since corruption was viewed as a symptom of underlying dysfunction of public institutions. The Bank has since been involved, either directly through anticorruption interventions or indirectly through public sector reform projects, in hundreds of projects in about 100 countries, encompassing public expenditure management, civil service and judicial reforms, tax policy, decentralization,

1999

Factoring Governance into Lending

Governance, including corruption and transparency, becomes part of the internal country assessment ratings, and factor into the lending allocations through the soft loan (IDA window).

Worldwide Governance Indicators

The Bank produces the Worldwide Governance Indicators for the first time and initiates the "Governance Matters" research series, distilling main lessons and findings on corruption and governance. The indicators are periodically updated and used worldwide.

e-government, service delivery, and direct anticorruption assistance. Bank lending for governance and public sector reform currently makes up about one-fifth of Bank projects, totaling about $4 billion a year. The breadth of coverage of governance-related projects is illustrated by judicial reforms in Albania and the Philippines, administrative reforms in Bolivia and Tanzania, customs modernization in Afghanistan, revenue system reforms in Bulgaria, and capacity building and institutional reforms in Ethiopia, Georgia, Ghana, Honduras, Latvia, Madagascar, Paraguay, and Uganda.

In some countries the work starts with empirical surveys, which gather in-depth information from the country's citizens, firms, and public officials. These surveys, which also include public expenditure tracking, enhance transparency and provide a diagnosis of the governance and anticorruption problems, and serve as a key input for an action program. The country then conducts national workshops with a broad spectrum of society to disseminate the findings and discuss recommendations for action. Governance and anticorruption strategies are then developed, supported by Bank and donor interventions.

Mainstreaming corruption considerations into the Bank's operational work

The Bank now explicitly considers in its lending decisions the extent to which the quality of governance and the magnitude of corruption affect a borrowing country's economy. The Bank's allocation formula for its recipients of soft loans (through the IDA concessional window) features the quality of governance as an important factor. And since 1999 the country assistance strategy (CAS) document is expected to examine governance

2000

High-Level Corruption and State Capture Measured

Analytical and empirical findings on state capture are published in *Seize the Day, Seize the State: Capture, Corruption, and Influence in Transition Economies,* addressing high-level corruption. It is an input to the United Nations Economic Commission for Africa report *Anticorruption in Transition.*

A Strategy for Strengthening Governance

The Bank releases *Reforming Public Institutions and Strengthening Governance: A World Bank Strategy.*

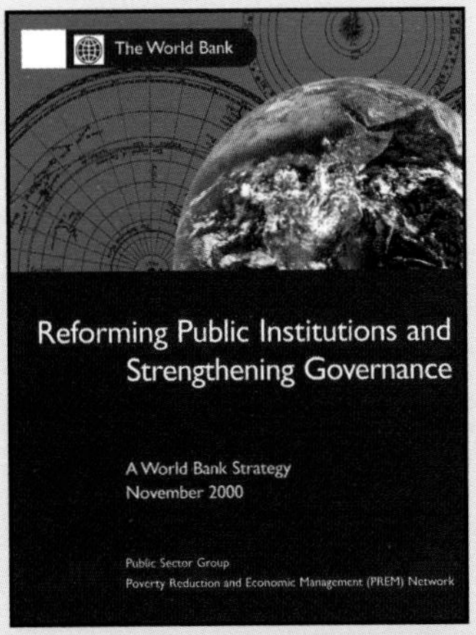

issues, including corruption. Some CASs stand out, featuring a frank discussion of the challenge, but follow through on the operational implications of analyzing the reality of governance and corruption in the country.

The Bank has started to focus on innovative programs working at the community level, while investing in the promotion of the demand side for good governance through work with civil society, operational research, technical assistance, and policy dialogue. In recent years work at the local level has multiplied, driven by a strategy of investing in a bottom-up approach to enhance voice and accountability. By the end of 2003 the Bank issued the first governance country assistance strategy, directing the Bank's activities to address the fundamental challenges of improving governance and controlling corruption.

Supporting international efforts to address corruption

Wolfensohn's 1996 address helped focus global attention on corruption, resulting in emphasis by other international financial institutions and improved information-sharing and collaboration. The five largest multilateral development banks established a joint working group to help coordination, while the Bank also strengthened its working relationships on this issue with UN agencies and bilateral donors. The Bank has also supported the OECD Antibribery Convention and the UN Anticorruption Convention, as well as contributing to international fora. And the Bank has developed close working relationships with many NGOs in client countries and with Transparency International.

The power of data

Underpinning much of the strategy work by the Bank and its assistance to countries has been the "power of data" and its analysis. Up to 10 years ago,

2001
Institutional Integrity
The Bank replaces the internal Anti-Corruption and Fraud Investigations Unit with the new Department of Institutional Integrity, entrusted with broadening its role in investigating claims of fraud and corruption within the institution and in Bank-funded projects.

2002
Building Institutions for Markets
The *World Development Report 2002: Building Institutions for Markets* emphasizes the importance of building institutions.

governance and corruption were topics regarded as unmeasurable, and where measurement was being tried, it was discounted as unreliable. Early on, Jim Wolfensohn supported the development of an empirical basis, at first due to the role of data in supporting the notion that corruption was a brake to development, and thereafter to monitor progress worldwide and derive lessons. He also supported an evidence-based approach to open up new "frontier" subjects related to governance, such as the empirical work done linking civil liberties and human rights with developmental outcomes, as well as the work on state capture by elites undermining governance.

Today, a very large and expanding Bank database on governance is publicly accessible, and its governance indicators—currently assessing governance in many dimensions for more than 200 countries—are issued periodically and widely used by reformists in government, civil society, policy analysis, and research. This evidence-based approach to governance and corruption, with its large governance databank, is key to assessing rigorously the successes and failures and to pointing to the vulnerabilities in the Bank's anticorruption strategy.

Indeed, from the evidence and lessons of experience some key challenges emerge for the next stage, as elaborated in the full paper mentioned at the outset:

- Further selectivity, with data as a guide.
- Further prioritization and operational focus at the country level (as illustrated by the Indonesia CAS).
- Proactively engaging with the private sector and multinationals.
- Concretely elevating the importance of governance and anticorruption among the G-7 and G-20.

Jim Wolfensohn shattered the taboo around discussion of the "c" word and in his public and private discourse helped to convince leaders all over the world that corruption was a deadly obstacle to development, and that it was far from inevitable.

Peter Eigen
Chairman
Transparency International

2003

Governance CAS

The Bank releases its first country assistance strategy anchored on governance and anticorruption, for Indonesia.

Reviewing Progress—Workshop with TI

A special workshop is held with Transparency International, assessing the Bank's efforts to combat corruption. The workshop highlights achievements and identifies key obstacles in attaining further progress, including the role of political determinants of corruption.

2004

A Force Against Corruption

The World Bank is financing anticorruption programs in more than 100 countries.

- Fully embracing the new innovations in transparency as key in the next generation of institutional and governance reforms.

Wolfensohn broke the taboo and unleashed a sea change on anticorruption at the Bank. Yet the international context has also changed, with recent positive and negative lessons not only from emerging markets, but also from Enron, Elf, Sarbanes-Oxley, Elliot Spitzer, and the UN Oil-for-Food program, among others. This also has implications for the challenges for the next stage.

2004
Increased Resources for Institutional Integrity
The Internal Investigators Department for Institutional Integrity, which has about 50 investigators, increases its budget to nearly $10 million.

2005
Report on Fraud and Corruption
The first Annual Report on the World Bank's investigation of fraud and corruption in Bank-funded projects is publicly issued, detailing how more than 300 firms and individuals have been publicly sanctioned, precluding them from procurement in Bank-funded contracts.

Part Two

LEVERAGING THROUGH PARTNERSHIPS

10

IN 1995 JIM WOLFENSOHN JOINED AN INSTITUTION UNDER SIEGE.

The "50 Years Is Enough" movement had gained traction across a broad swath of civil society and the media with its argument, on the occasion of the Bank's 50th anniversary, that the multilateral organization was doing more harm than good for development and should, consequently, close its doors. The Bank-IMF Annual Meetings held in Madrid in the fall of 1994 were overshadowed by mass protests in the streets and public criticisms of the Bretton Woods institutions—the beginning of the antiglobalization movement that would persist through the rest of the 1990s.

For the Bank the nadir was when protesters interrupted the opening Annual Meetings press conference in Madrid by Lew Preston, president of the Bank at the time. The same was true of Preston's Annual Meetings address: Greenpeace activists infiltrated the conference hall where the meetings were taking place and interrupted the proceedings by swinging down from the ceiling, showering fake banknotes on the delegates, and chanting pro-environment, anti-Bank slogans.

Preston had recognized the need for the Bank to improve its external image. He often complained about the Bank's "inward-looking" and arrogant culture that seemed to make it impervious to criticism. When Wolfensohn arrived, he took action to change things.

All of his personal instincts were geared toward outreach and partnership with others. Before coming to the Bank, in his private business as an investment advisor, he had been nicknamed by some as "the man with the golden Rolodex"—such was the scope of his personal contacts. In many ways, he was the ultimate "relationship" banker.

1995
Opening Up the Bank
In his first Annual Meetings address, Wolfensohn sends clear signals that the Bank is changing. It will be listening more and opening up to a new, much broader development agenda—one that simply could not be achieved without partners.

1996
Mainstreaming Participation
The World Bank launches its *Participation Sourcebook* for staff.

To be a good partner, we must be ready to listen to criticism and respond to constructive comment. There is no place for arrogance in the development business. I want to have a Bank that is open and ready to learn from others and that holds itself accountable.

James D. Wolfensohn
Washington, D.C.
October 10, 1995

In the months before he joined the Bank, he read all of its major critiques—on issues of environment, structural adjustment, debt, and the impact of its programs on poor people. Visitors to his home in the summer of 1995 saw the desk in his study piled high with NGO tracts against the Bank. He wanted to understand the source of the fierce criticisms against the institution he was about to lead.

In developing his business strategy for transforming the Bank, he knew that he had to take into account the changing environment in which it operated. He was convinced that the Bank could not survive in an introverted, hunkered-down mode. It needed to reach out, to friends and foes alike.

Wolfensohn understood that in the modern world of the Internet and instant knowledge exchange, no institution can operate effectively by acting in isolation. The days when the Bank could rely on its position as a monopolist provider of financial resources to the developing countries were gone. The Bank now needed to be responsive to the global-market test. It needed to be trusted by its clients. It needed to shake off its image of being arrogant and elitist and get closer to its clients and the people of their countries.

In his first months in the job, Wolfensohn sent clear signals that times had changed at the Bank—that it was going to listen more to others. (Perhaps the charge made most often against the pre-Wolfensohn Bank was that it did not "listen.")

One major act was to initiate a discussion on debt relief for the poorest countries, a discussion which, up to that point, the Bank had refused to countenance. This led to the establishment of the Heavily Indebted Poor Countries Initiative and over $50 billion in debt relief for the developing nations.

1998
Interfaith Dialogue
Wolfensohn and the Archbishop of Canterbury host a dialogue with leaders of faith-based organizations, launching an initiative to strengthen and scale up the global fight against poverty, build on the sense of common purpose and commitment, and advance the dialogue on the development agenda.

Jim Wolfensohn . . . transformed the Bank from a faceless, detested, and feared institution, subject to much criticism, to a more humane Bank that in the last 10 years has become very much associated with the poor.

José Ramos-Hotra
Nobel Peace Prize
Laureate (1996)

A second major act, in 1996, was the announcement during his second Annual Meetings address that corruption was a cancer on the face of development and must be addressed. Many of his senior advisors had argued that he should not talk about the "c" word. Anticorruption and governance were to become hallmarks of the Bank's future programs.

These early acts sent a clear message that the Bank was changing. It was listening. It was opening to a new, much broader development agenda—one that simply could not be achieved without partners. This was a profound change for an organization that had for decades prided itself on "going it alone." Wolfensohn, in effect, changed the culture toward consultation and partnership—the pinnacle of which was perhaps the adoption of the Comprehensive Development Framework, which embedded the notion of partnership in all the institution's development work at the country level. The same could be said of the Poverty Reduction Strategy Papers, which embedded consultation as a new way of doing business.

One of the most revolutionary signals Wolfensohn sent about the opening of the Bank was his early decision to decentralize the institution on a major scale. Before his arrival at the Bank, senior managers had been debating endlessly the pros and cons of decentralization—that is, more Bank staff should live and work in the countries they are supporting. Wolfensohn cut quickly to the chase: the Bank was going to decentralize and put its country directors and many other staff in the field to get closer to clients and to make the Bank's operations more effective. Despite some internal criticisms it proved to be one of his best and highest impact decisions. In 1995 the Bank had none of its country directors in the field; by 2005, 73 percent of its country directors were in the field, as were a

1999
Comprehensive Development Framework
The CDF is launched, embodying the changed culture toward consultation and partnership in all the institution's development work at the country level and laying the foundation for the later adoption of the Poverty Reduction Strategy Paper approach.

third of its entire regional staff. Partly as a result, the Bank's effectiveness ratings went up.

Driven by Wolfensohn, the Bank revitalized its relationships with the world in the period 1995–2005 and in the process became a more trusted, more effective, and, above all, more relevant organization. A "global poll" of opinion leaders across the world undertaken in 2003 testified as much—while also indicating that more progress was still needed.

Besides reinventing its relationships with clients through decentralization, Wolfensohn's Bank revamped its connections with other groups:

- *The UN and other international financial institutions.* Forming a virtual "multilateral development bank club," the Bank led substantive efforts to harmonize and coordinate policies and programs for more effective delivery to clients.
- *Civil society.* There was no overnight turnaround, and many NGOs in particular continue to be strident critics of the Bank (including continuing to protest the Bank's Annual Meetings). But by 2005 there was civil society participation in 70 percent of Bank projects, and largely through the Bank's advocacy, civil society had become a major voice in developing countries' development plans (Wolfensohn designated staff as specific civil society "focal points" in most of the Bank's country offices).
- *The private sector.* Partnerships grew in areas of the environment (carbon funds), corporate social responsibility, and in the approach to the development of extractive industries.
- *Parliamentarians.* A major and influential group, parliamentarians—thus far ignored by the Bank—became an important network that met to discuss and lend support to development issues.

2001
Transparency in Operations
The World Bank Board adopts a new disclosure policy.

2002
Partnership with Civil Society
Wolfensohn addresses a forum hosted by the NGO umbrella group InterAction on the need to translate Monterrey pledges into action.

In the communications age, Wolfensohn also understood well the power of technology and the media. He made a major investment in transforming the Bank into a modern business, with its global offices connected on a 24/7 basis and numerous videoconferences taking place daily. In addition, in all of his many country visits, he not only made speeches and met with the new constituencies that the Bank was developing, but he invariably spent time with the press—with an amazing capacity to answer any question on any detail of a project or a country, rebutting out-of-date criticisms, explaining the Bank's new approaches, and repositioning the institution in the public eye.

A natural communicator himself—his speechmaking ability was prodigious—Wolfensohn also pushed the introverted Bank and its staff to become extroverted and to reach out more to the outside world: to become more comfortable with transparency, public scrutiny, and accountability; to become more comfortable with real dialogue; to become more comfortable with listening.

One other important aspect of opening the Bank was Wolfensohn's huge effort to break down the organization's internal bureaucracy and make the institutional environment more "human." Before Wolfensohn, presidents of the Bank had been somewhat remote and aloof figures who resided on the 12th floor of the headquarters building in Washington, D.C., and were rarely seen by staff. Wolfensohn changed that in dramatic fashion. On his first day in office, he had a town hall meeting with staff—the first of many throughout his tenure—and he invited staff to be in direct contact with him through e-mail. Whenever he traveled, he always met with country-based staff.

Relations between the president and the staff were not always smooth while the institution went through such a massive period of change and

2003
Listening to Civil Society Organizations
Wolfensohn holds a town hall meeting with CSOs to hear their views.

upheaval. There were disagreements and, on some issues, confrontations. But there is no question that, well into his second term (2000–05), many staff felt a strong and almost personal connection with their leader. The all-staff surveys taken in 2003 and 2004 indicated significant leaps in morale, with more than 90 percent indicating that they were "proud" to work at the Bank.

By 2005 the Bank was probably the world's most "networked" international organization, at the center of the global development process, and recognized once more as the world's premier development institution. Thanks to Wolfensohn's belief in outreach, the Bank was once again empowered to be the leading voice on global development issues.

Perhaps one of the most the most telling signals of Wolfensohn's success was the night in May 2004—10 years after the debacle in Madrid—when Greenpeace once again interacted directly with the World Bank. This time, however, its members did not hang from the ceilings shouting their protests at the Bank's president. Instead, Wolfensohn, at Greenpeace's invitation, addressed its annual meeting in London.

When he finished speaking, he was given a warm ovation.

Under Wolfensohn's leadership, the Bank grew in size and scope, once again becoming the preeminent global economic development institution that it once was. . . He used the Bank as a bully pulpit to declare institutional war on global poverty and released its resources on improving education and health care, as well as promoting equality for women, in developing countries. Wolfensohn gave voice to the world's poor, integrating their views into the Bank's planning. And in the process, he defused many of the institution's most vociferous critics.

National Journal
January 2005

2005
Decentralized Bank
From having no country directors in the field in 1995, the Bank now has 73 percent of its country directors in country offices.

11

THE BANK, OFTEN DESCRIBED BEFORE 1995 AS INTROVERTED, NEVERTHELESS had ties with other multilateral institutions, the United Nations, businesses, some civil society organizations, and several major foundations. But under Jim Wolfensohn, the Bank's strategic alliances with others literally exploded, and many previously ignored constituencies started interacting with the institution. In the space of 10 years the Bank became the most extroverted and most strategically networked of all multilaterals, involved in hundreds of partnerships. To illustrate what this has really meant, it is best to let the examples speak for themselves.

Partnering with developed and developing countries

Ties between the Bank and developed countries became much more intense, as Wolfensohn made up to 20 visits a year, around the world from New Zealand to Canada to Japan to Europe—each time engaging multiple interlocutors, from the heads of state or governments down to ministries, local civil society, business, and the media. With Europe representing about half of ODA and of IDA, Wolfensohn set up a small vice presidency for Europe. It helped boost the Bank-Europe links across the board, from getting Italy to finance e-government to mobilizing European development ministers around the Comprehensive Development Framework idea or getting the EU institutions to embrace the Poverty Reduction Strategy Paper process now being implemented in more than 50 countries. The Bank also started highly productive partnerships with regions in Europe (Bavaria, North Rhine-Westphalia, Campania, Catalonia, and so on) as well as cities' and mayors' networks—reflecting the interesting new trend of increasing involvement by subnational entities in development activities.

1995
Partnerships as a Core Theme
In his first Annual Meetings address, Wolfensohn outlines partnerships as one of the core themes that will carry through his presidency.

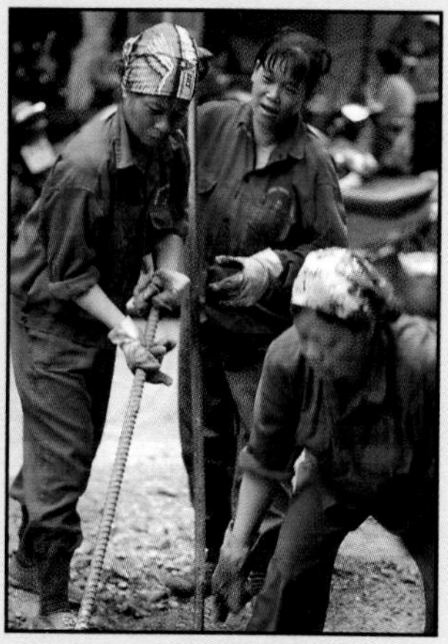

1996
Stronger Partnership with the IMF
Weekly breakfasts start between the IMF and World Bank heads.

The result of these multiple developed-country links is that, unlike the Bank before 1995, the institution now possesses a considerable portfolio of developed country relationships and links—an asset the next World Bank president will be able to continue to exploit for the causes of poverty reduction and development. Another result of these partnering efforts with the developed world is the explosion in Bank-managed trust funds across a very large range of topics, many of them addressing burning global issues. The Bank also is now often part of G-20, G-7 Finance, and G-8 meetings, a rarity in the Bank before 1995.

Developing countries are, of course, natural partners of the Bank—but here, too, efforts during the Wolfensohn years gave this idea special meaning and heft. For one, the notion of partnership figured prominently in the philosophy and designs of the Comprehensive Development Framework and the Poverty Reduction Strategy Papers. Second, Wolfensohn battled endlessly for the idea of a two-way partnership between developed-country donors and developing-country governments—the "two-way bargain" that he kept insisting on speech after speech, before and after the Monterrey Summit. And third, many new partnerships were struck on the ground, often with original vehicles or venues. If one had to pick one vignette of this partnership spirit, it would be the early sessions where Wolfensohn would huddle with a score of African heads of state to brainstorm over the main issues facing the region. Or the example of the Bank-created Global Development Learning Network with its 70-odd classrooms being used by all kinds of content partners to create communities of practice for developing-country officials battling with the same issue, 10–15 countries at a time. Or the unflagging support to the pioneers of the New Partnership for Africa's Development.

1997

Stronger Partnerships with Business and NGOs

First steps are taken in the Business Partnership for Development Program, with the piloting of some 30 trisector partnerships on the ground.

Partnering with other international organizations

Even before the 1997/98 financial crisis, Jim Wolfensohn pushed for much closer ties with its sister institution, the International Monetary Fund. Weekly breakfast meetings would see the heads of the two institutions go through checklists of joint issues. For the benefit of many countries, the two institutions started a multicountry joint Financial Sector Assessment Program, and teamed up on debt relief (the Heavily Indebted Poor Countries Initiative), on Poverty Reduction Strategy Papers, and on debt sustainability issues (there are now more than six such joint Bank-Fund programs). Nineteenth Street became narrower somehow, and tensions became rarer.

Similarly, the Bank-UN ties grew stronger. The links with the Secretary-General became personal and close, especially under Kofi Annan and when the Bank's own Mark Malloch Brown took over the helm of the UNDP. At all levels, and across the 40-odd UN agencies and programs, Bank-UN alliances bloomed, especially in the health, AIDS, postconflict, and environmental areas. In addition to the Bank's New York office, Wolfensohn reopened the offices in Geneva in 2000. The result is that despite some occasional frictions, the Bank has become much more of a UN family member.

The Bank also started forming with the other regional development banks an unprecedented multilateral development bank club. Building on the many operational ties among them, a rich process of regular joint multilateral development bank meetings on procurement, financial management, evaluation, and many other topics has been launched—in a manner typical of the Wolfensohn partnership philosophy, with other institutions in the lead where they are best suited for this.

1998

Partnership with Industrial Countries

Wolfensohn creates a vice presidency for Europe, with its headquarters in Paris and offices in Brussels, London, Rome, and Frankfurt, with the aims of bringing Europe and the World Bank closer to each other and of developing the Bank's synergies with the EU institutions, the OECD, and other Europe-based players.

2000

Partnership with OECD

A joint statement by the World Bank and OECD provides a broad and flexible framework for cooperation and collaboration between the institutions, with the following areas as priorities for cooperation: development partnerships and goals, corporate governance, combating corruption, social sectors, sustainable development, environment, and knowledge-based economies.

Ties with the World Trade Organization, boosted through the reopening of the Geneva offices, span many areas. With the OECD's secretary-general, Wolfensohn entered a broad collaboration agreement, now spanning some 20 key topics. The Bank is involved in seven of the OECD's committees, including a strategic alliance between the Bank and the OECD's Development Assistance Committee that is one of the main forces for aid effectiveness and harmonization. The partnerships with the European Commission and the European Investment Bank have also flourished, with several important collaboration agreements for key regions, a surge in trust fund activities, and regular meetings facilitated by a busy Brussels office.

Partnering with global constituencies

The Bank's best-known and most controversial partnership effort during these 10 years may well have been that with civil society—with operational NGOs, advocacy NGOs, foundations, and so on. Whatever the debate about these ties, and notwithstanding the NGO world's continuing role as occasional critic, the upshot is that more than 70 percent of the Bank's projects now involve NGOs or community-based organizations of beneficiaries in their execution, that all the Bank Group's strategies and policies now benefit from civil society consultations, and that on many global issues civil society and the Bank have teamed up in ways that would have struck earlier Bank presidents as amazing. At any rate, the much-increased horsepower behind such big causes as the need for substantial ODA increases, for more development-oriented trade negotiations, and for much bigger resources for HIV/AIDS, has been a direct result of this engagement.

2000

Stronger Partnership with the UN
The first-ever address by a World Bank president to the UN Security Council takes place. The Bank reopens an office in Geneva after a long absence, cementing the Bank's relationship as a member of the UN family.

Partnership with Parliamentarians
The World Bank and members of parliaments create the Parliamentary Network on the World Bank. Started in Europe, this now-independent international network of about 800 members from 110 developed and developing countries goes global.

THE BANK AND CIVIL SOCIETY—PROGRESS IN EMPOWERMENT

The Bank's expansive and varied engagement with CSOs around the globe as of 2005 reflects civil society's growing role in development assistance, as well as lessons learned by the Bank about the importance of citizen empowerment to poverty reduction and development effectiveness. OECD estimates that CSOs handle at least $12 billion annually in international relief and development aid, making them a major player in development finance.

Since his arrival in 1995, Jim Wolfensohn encouraged the Bank to expand its outreach to civil society, recognizing that CSOs can help promote good governance, build public consensus and local ownership for reforms, extend service delivery into grassroots communities or other areas where it is harder for the Bank and other donors to reach, identify and manage risks, and make development more sustainable. Whereas engaging with CSOs was once seen as less than crucial, the Bank's member countries now agree that engaging CSOs is a key factor in helping reach the Millennium Development Goals.

Among the countless and innovative examples of Bank–civil society engagement are:

- Channeling about half the Bank's funds for the Multi-Country HIV/AIDS Program to CSOs in over 20,000 AIDS treatment, surveillance, prevention, and education programs.
- Working with a coalition of CSOs, local governments, and donor agencies to train CSOs in Africa, Latin America, and Asia on how to track and monitor government spending and how to improve the public's understanding of the budget process so they can hold their elected officials accountable.
- Partnering with women's federations in rural China to improve their communities' livelihoods, promote women's empowerment, and close the gender gap.
- Managing a social fund in West Bank and Gaza that enables Palestinian CSOs to provide jobs and social services to the local population and strengthens the role of the CSOs in advocacy and policy reforms.

Over the past decade, promoting civic engagement has become part of the Bank's basic business model, with focal points in headquarters and in country offices, and nearly all operational staff are involved with CSOs in their daily work. Regular dialogue and consultation take place on Bank-financed projects as well as on nearly every major issue, strategy, or policy change at the global, national, and local level. Several hundred CSO representatives attend and participate in dialogues at the Bank's Annual Meetings—a far cry from 10 years ago.

Of course, many CSOs who are partners or allies of the Bank may also be critics on specific issues—but they are willing to engage with a Bank that is more open to listening to their views. And the Bank has learned that such criticisms can be beneficial. For example, CSO advocacy has been instrumental in pressuring for greater debt relief and aid flows, environmental and social safeguards, information disclosure, monitoring and evaluation, and focus on poverty impacts. With 184 member countries, each with its unique context for civic participation, the Bank's challenge going forward is to promote best practices for engaging with CSOs across countries and to ensure greater coordination, coherence, and accountability.

—Carolyn Reynolds

Partnerships with the private sector were also a prominent feature in the Wolfensohn tenure. The International Finance Corporation increased the level of its private sector activities considerably from $2.1 billion in commitments in fiscal 1996 to $4.75 billion in fiscal 2004, and moved further toward frontier markets. The Multilateral Investment Guarantee Agency's operations soared. By contrast, the Bank started around 1998 to reduce its infrastructure activities (only to increase them again lately), thus disappointing many private sector players.

But against this backdrop, many new types of Bank-business partnerships bloomed:

- The International Finance Corporation's Equator Principles.
- The Business Partnership for Development trisector partnership experiment.
- Collaboration with the business world through such new tools as carbon trading funds or trust funds now open to private donations (InfoDev, the World Bank Institute, the Consultative Group to Aid the Poor, the Consultative Group on International Agricultural Research).
- Regularly held CEO forums.
- Efforts to unleash the new informatics and communications technologies for development.
- The 40 or so private sector liaison officers working with the Bank group in as many countries.
- The brilliant, private sector–inspired development marketplace contest.
- And many other examples.

But a less-known but equally interesting facet of the Wolfensohn era may well be the opening to other constituencies never engaged before. Links

2001
Stronger Partnerships with Clients
Wolfensohn holds a meeting with 12 African heads of state in Dar-es-Salaam, Tanzania, to discuss how to move Africa to the top of the 21st century's development agenda.

2003
Inclusion of Civil Society
As part of the Annual Meetings, Wolfensohn participates in a town hall with civil society organizations, joined by IMF managing director Horst Kohler and key finance officials from around the globe. More than 70 percent of Bank projects now involve civil society organizations.

with parliamentarians bloomed through the now 800-strong Parliamentary Network on the World Bank, started in Europe but now globally deployed with regional chapters, annual conferences, and study tours. The World Bank Institute provided training on oversight to some 3,000 members of parliament from the developing world. And borrower countries now increasingly rope their parliamentarians into PRSP discussions on the ground. No other international financial institution has made such an effort.

Under Jim Wolfensohn, the Bank also started to team up with youth from all over the world in the development agenda. Annual meetings with youth organization leaders, for example, focus on dangerous behaviors, youth employment, and conflict issues. These organizations have 220 million members in the developing world, many of which now connect to Bank offices and programs in their respective countries.

Academics, traditionally both an important and often critical audience, are now engaged in more systematically organized partnerships with the Bank—through the big Annual World Bank Conferences on Development Economics in Europe and throughout the world, through the Global Development Network consortium with more than 700 members, and through a much greater opening of the Bank's Development Economics vice presidency research arm to the world of external researchers, think tanks, universities, and the like.

The Wolfensohn Bank opened relations with more than 30 faith leaders from all creeds and corners of the world, on the often misunderstood but obvious recognition that faiths and their faith-based NGOs are, just like the Bank, both a major lobbying force for a better world and a major actor on the ground. The Bank-faith synergies are therefore potentially

Partnering with the Private Sector

By engaging with major investment banks responsible for 80 percent of project financing in emerging markets, the International Finance Corporation persuades these institutions to sign up to its own environmental and social standards, under the banner of the Equator Principles.

2004

Collaborating with Youth

Wolfensohn travels to Sarajevo for the Second Conference on Youth, Development, and Peace, to gather input from representatives of more than 100 youth organizations on development issues and to identify opportunities for further cooperation between youth organizations and the World Bank.

very powerful—whatever one thinks about the need for secular distance. For similar reasons Jim Wolfensohn was also the first president to hold regular dialogues with the trade union movements.

Facile critics may deplore this proliferation of initiatives. But the critics may have failed to see just how important it is to give the institution a triple raison d'être: resource transfer, knowledge sharing, and partnership platform. The Bank stands stronger on these three feet, and Jim Wolfensohn is the one who had this vision—one in which partnerships and strategic alliances are not occasional extras, but a central part of the Bank Group's role in the world's agenda for poverty reduction, development, and environmental sustainability.

2005
Global Programs and Partnerships
In a reflection of the growth in global programs and partnerships over the past decade, the amount of donor funds held in trust increased to $8.6 billion in 2005, up from $2.1 billion in 1995.

12

In 1995, the year Jim Wolfensohn took the helm of the World Bank, official development assistance (ODA) amounted to $45 billion, substantially below the levels of the early 1990s in nominal and real terms. As the 1995 *World Debt Tables* noted, "Among DAC [Development Assistance Committee] members, ODA as a share of GNP fell to a weighted average of 0.27 percent, its lowest level in 45 years." This trend of shrinking aid continued through the rest of the 1990s with official aid declining in real terms, and falling to only 0.21 percent of donor GNP by 2001.

Shrinking aid

As described in chapter 7, much of the attention of the international community in the second half of the 1990s was focused on debt relief for the poorest countries. These efforts reduced the large debt overhangs of these countries, but there was no increase in net resources for development finance. From the beginning, Jim Wolfensohn stressed that debt relief should be additional and should not displace much-needed ODA to finance long-term development. Aggregate ODA continued to shrink, however, with a growing portion being used to fund activities other than long-term development, such as emergency relief and peacekeeping. Within this declining pool of ODA, net transfers to the heavily indebted poor countries (HIPC) did not fall by as much as for other low-income countries.

The onset of the East Asian financial crisis in 1997 and the subsequent wave of financial crises in emerging markets provoked a new concern that aid might be diverted away from the poorest countries. The Bank and the international community provided large financial support to the affected countries, but most of this was nonconcessional lending.

1996
IDA11
The World Bank and donors successfully conclude the 11th round of IDA negotiations, resulting in a $19.2 billion replenishment for the next three years.

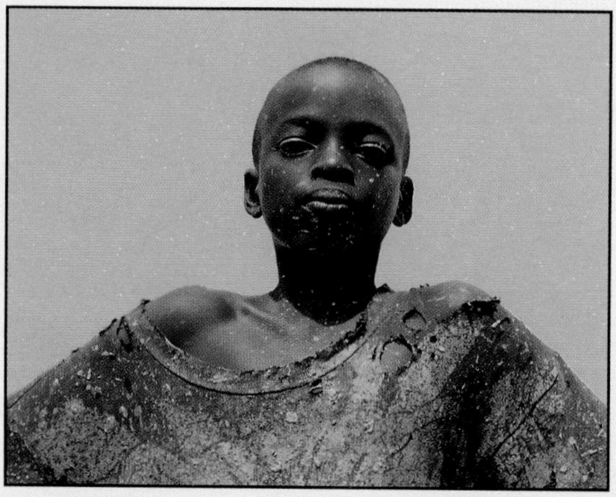

Against this background of shrinking aid and tight budgets, the 1990s proved to be a testing period for IDA replenishments. IDA10, which covered the period 1994–96, was threatened by cuts in donor budgets, with some predicting that it would be the "last IDA." As a result of the strenuous efforts and leadership of Jim Wolfensohn, IDA was able to garner continued donor support, albeit without any substantial increase from the levels of IDA10. It was only in 2005 with IDA14 that increased donor pledges allowed for a substantial increase in the IDA envelope ($34 billion from an average of $22.5 billion in IDA10 through IDA13), and higher concessionality in the form of grants for the poorest and most vulnerable countries.

Assessing aid effectiveness

In the late 1990s, a new body of research, much of it in the Bank, sparked a new focus and debate on aid effectiveness. Some used the findings of research on aid effectiveness to argue that most aid had been ineffective and that aid was not an essential ingredient for success. In the lead up to and since Monterrey, Wolfensohn led the Bank in making the case that there had been remarkable development progress over the past 50 years—and that although not always well targeted or well used, aid in terms of money and ideas had made an important contribution to that development.

Wolfensohn brought perspective and balance to the debate on aid's selectivity. He was the first to stress the importance of sound policies and good institutions for the effective use of aid. He was also the first to stress that the Bank and the international community could not simply ignore countries that lacked these conditions. With his urging and under his leadership, the Bank launched the Low-Income Countries Under Stress Initiative, which

1998
Linking Governance and Aid Effectiveness
The Bank publishes *Assessing Aid: What Works, What Doesn't, and Why,* which argues that aid is more effective in countries with good policies in place.

1999
Adoption of PRSPs
The World Bank and IMF adopt nationally owned participatory Poverty Reduction Strategy Papers as the basis for all World Bank and IMF concessional lending.

IDA12
IDA funds are increased to $20.5 billion in the 12th replenishment by donors for 2000–02.

has broadened into a global effort to find the best means to support development needs and catalyze change in weak performers and fragile states.

Wolfensohn also brought balance to the discussion on what the developing country recipients and what the donor community needs to do. He urged developing country leaders to tackle the weaknesses that inhibited development, pointing to the need to strengthen governance and tackle corruption and to the high costs and lack of coordination in the donor community. And he stressed the need for reform on the part of both multilateral and bilateral partners. He pressed for and supported internal reforms in the Bank so that it would be a better aid partner, and he worked with his fellow multilateral development bank presidents to improve the effectiveness of development support from the multilateral institutions. But he also pressed the Bank and the Development Assistance Committee of the OECD for more rigorous analysis of bilateral aid, work showing that only a small proportion of bilateral aid is made available as cash financing to support projects and programs in recipient countries.

Mobilizing more aid

The Monterrey Conference on Financing for Development was an important turning point in the commitment of donor countries to increase aid financing after more than a decade of decline. In the lead up to and since Monterrey, Wolfensohn canvassed hard with the G-7 and other developed countries to step up their commitments to make the Monterrey Consensus a success. These efforts paid good dividends as key donors came forward with pledges for substantial increases in their aid commitments.

As a result the trend in official development assistance has reversed, rising from \$52 billion in 2001 to \$78 billion in 2004. Although the real increase

2001

A Millennial Challenge

The World Bank commits itself as a full partner to the UN in the implementation of the Millennium Development Goals adopted by the international community in the United Nations Millennium Declaration.

2002

A Case for Aid

Building a Consensus for Development Assistance is published by the Bank. The book makes the case for aid by drawing lessons from World Bank experience. It includes a keynote speech given two weeks before the Monterrey Conference by Wolfensohn which crystallizes the key challenges and the opportunities faced by the international community.

New Aid Partnership

At the Monterrey Conference on Financing for Development, Jim Wolfensohn rallies donors to mobilize the additional \$40–\$60 billion a year needed to achieve the Millennium Development Goals.

IDA Grants

IDA13 is successfully concluded, boosting IDA funds to \$23 billion for the next three years, with about 20 percent set aside as grants for the first time.

is much smaller, and although a large proportion of this increase was for debt relief, technical cooperation, and countries affected by conflict, the reversal in aid was a milestone in development cooperation.

Nevertheless, the amount of aid is far short of what poor countries need and can use productively. Jim Wolfensohn has joined Gordon Brown and others in calling for at least a doubling of aid. Citing the shortfall of financing for the Education for All Fast-Track Initiative, he has argued that adequate and predictable aid was key in helping the poorest countries scale up efforts to meet the Millennium Development Goals.

He has been a constant champion of further progress toward the ODA target of 0.7 percent of gross national income target in order to meet the growing financing needs. Since Monterrey, six countries have committed to meet the 0.7 percent target, in addition to the five that have already reached the target. Since existing commitments to increase aid as well as efforts to increase aid levels further will take time, Wolfensohn has supported efforts to complement increased aid flows and commitments with innovative mechanisms. The Bank and the Fund have been working to help the international community consider and take forward such innovative mechanisms as the International Finance Facility, global taxes, enhanced voluntary contributions, and blending arrangements.

Improving aid quality

Wolfensohn's leadership paved the way for the Rome High-Level Forum on Harmonization in 2003 and the Marrakech Roundtable on Managing for Development Results in 2004, bringing together all stakeholders—bilateral agencies, multilateral institutions, and developing country partners—to address the

2003
Harmonization and Results
At the Rome High-Level Forum on Harmonization, the Bank joins other participants in committing to greater harmonization, encouraging country ownership, and focusing on implementation at the country level.

2004
Donors Respond
Official development assistance rises to $78 billion, from $52 billion in 2001, albeit with little increase in cash financing for the poorest countries.

THE INTERNATIONAL DEVELOPMENT ASSOCIATION

The International Development Association (IDA) was established in 1960 to support the efforts of the world's poorest countries to reduce poverty, improve living conditions, and boost economic growth. IDA relies on donor funding to provide concessional loans and grants to 81 low-income countries. IDA commitments have grown significantly over the past decade and are projected to increase to about $11 billion annually by 2006. IDA, a leader in the international effort to progress toward the Millennium Development Goals, is a lifeline for many of the world's poorest people.

IDA has undergone important changes over the past 10 years, reflecting changes in the external environment and lessons from experience and research. This period saw a recommitment to the overarching goal of poverty reduction, including by supporting countries in their efforts to provide basic social services to their citizens, strengthening governance and tackling corruption, pursuing policies that promote growth, and working more closely with all its development partners, especially through the implementation of the principles contained in the Comprehensive Development Framework introduced in 1999 and operationalized through Poverty Reduction Strategy Papers.

To increase the overall effectiveness of its resources, IDA significantly enhanced the link between country performance and the level of IDA financial support during this period, giving greater weight to governance, environmental factors, nondevelopment expenditures, and IDA portfolio performance. IDA also introduced a new methodology for allocating resources to countries emerging from conflict to ensure adequate funding for their reconstruction and reconciliation efforts. It responded to calls for more transparency in the allocation process by agreeing to make public the country ratings on which allocations are based starting in fiscal 2006. Increased public scrutiny of these ratings should enhance the robustness and accuracy of these ratings and thus further increase IDA's effectiveness. Its leadership in this area has been widely recognized, and many development agencies now use allocation systems patterned after IDA's.

IDA has also incorporated a much stronger focus on ensuring that its operations achieve their intended results. During the IDA13 period (fiscal 2003–05) a special framework for monitoring results was introduced; this framework has been further strengthened in the recently agreed 14th replenishment of IDA, which calls for the monitoring of both aggregate country outcomes and IDA's contribution to these outcomes.

These changes, and many others introduced over the past 10 years, have strengthened IDA's capacity to assist low-income countries in their efforts to improve the quality of life of their citizens. As indicated by the substantial increase in funding that forms part of the IDA14 agreement (SDR 21.9 billion for IDA14, up from SDR 14.6 billion for IDA11). IDA is the cornerstone of the international community's efforts to combat global poverty.

—Geoffrey B. Lamb

MORE EFFECTIVE SUPPORT FOR MIDDLE-INCOME COUNTRIES

The rationale for enhanced Bank support to middle-income countries—defined by the Bank as countries eligible for IBRD lending—derives from the importance of sustained growth and poverty reduction in these countries, home to more than 70 percent of the developing world's poor, for achieving the global development goals and the Millennium Development Goals. Specifically, the Bank is uniquely placed to help middle-income countries in such key areas as institutional reform, infrastructure investment across the public-private spectrum, improved social-service delivery, and coping with market volatility. Supporting middle-income countries is an essential part of the Bank's commitment to the post-Monterrey global development agenda, complementing the institution's support to low-income countries and low-income countries under stress.

On average, middle-income countries have performed well in recent years, reflecting strengthened policies. But average performance conceals a very diverse picture, and nearly all middle-income countries face difficult development challenges.

- While some countries have been extremely successful, others have been much less so. Indeed a sizable number of middle-income countries have been so unsuccessful that they have reverted to low-income status.
- Sustained poverty reduction remains a challenge in most middle-income countries. Two billion people, or roughly half the population in middle-income countries, live on incomes of less than $2 a day. Substantial income inequality and social exclusion are also issues in many middle-income countries.
- Over the next 25 years, middle-income countries will account for 1.5 billion of the net 2 billion increase in world population.

In short, there is a large, unfinished development agenda in nearly all middle-income countries, albeit an agenda that differs widely between countries. Only very few middle-income countries are close to graduation to advanced country status requiring no support. To facilitate its support to middle-income countries, the Bank is implementing an action plan focusing on five main areas:

- Strengthening the ability of staff to respond to the development needs of middle-income countries. This includes initiatives to use countries' own safeguard and fiduciary systems where they are equivalent to the Bank's policy requirements; to further streamline policy conditionality in Bank operations; to make greater use of the inherent flexibility of the country assistance strategy framework to customize support to country circumstances and respond quickly to newly emerging lending opportunities; and to realign particular investment lending instruments and disbursement mechanisms with the evolving needs of clients.
- Making better use of Bank resources and skills to provide timely, relevant, and high-quality knowledge services.
- Strengthening support for risk management through better dissemination of existing IBRD products and development of new financial products.
- Exploiting Bank Group synergies, including lending and technical and analytical support to sub-sovereigns and through financial intermediaries.
- Enhancing partnerships with bilateral donors and multilateral agencies in supporting the development efforts of middle-income countries.

—R. Pablo Guerrero O.

aid effectiveness agenda through better alignment and harmonization and an enhanced focus on results.

Since then, the Bank has worked closely with the Development Assistance Committee of the OECD on its Working Party on Aid Practices to take forward this agenda. And these efforts, in turn, paved the way for the second High-Level Forum on Harmonization in Paris in 2005. The subtitle of the Paris Declaration—"Ownership, Harmonization, Alignment, Results, and Mutual Accountability"—captures the progress on shared objectives, and the efforts under way to specify indicators, timetables, and targets and to monitor and evaluate implementation can provide the basis of translating these objectives into tangible results.

Toward a new aid architecture

As a result of the discussions and collective efforts of the past few years, a new aid architecture is beginning to take shape. At its core are the Millennium Development Goals, common aspirations for building a development partnership. There is also broad consensus that this partnership must be based on a country-driven, country-owned approach, embodied in the poverty reduction strategy process for low-income countries.

As underscored by the Monterrey Consensus, financing for development encompasses many different elements requiring actions on the part of all partners, with a sharper focus on results, based on mutual accountability. Developing countries must take the lead in articulating and implementing strategies that aim higher through actions to spur economic growth, scale up human development services, and attract foreign direct investment. Developed countries, in addition to dismantling barriers to trade, need to substantially increase the level and effectiveness of aid.

2005

A Vote of Confidence in IDA

Negotiations for IDA14 result in a 30 percent increase in IDA, the largest boost in more than two decades and a 50 percent increase from IDA11, including an increased share allocated to grants for HIPC Initiative countries started under IDA13.

Harmonization, Alignment, and Results

The participants to the Paris High-Level Forum on Harmonization, Alignment, and Results commit their institutions and countries to continuing and increasing efforts in harmonization, alignment, and managing for results and list a set of monitorable actions and indicators to accelerate progress in these areas.

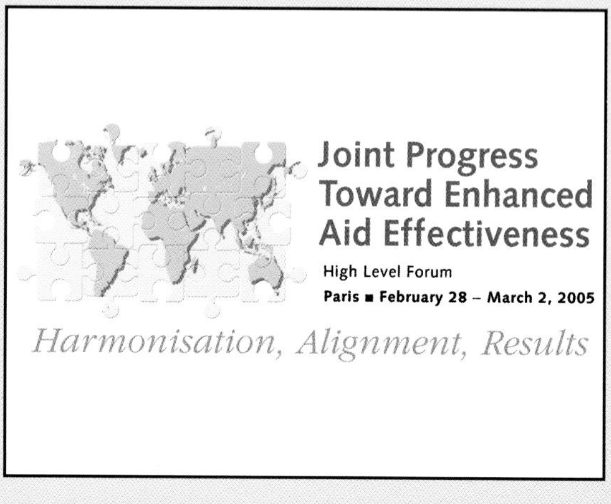

Joint Progress Toward Enhanced Aid Effectiveness
High Level Forum
Paris ■ February 28 – March 2, 2005
Harmonisation, Alignment, Results

Part Three

RENEWING THE INSTITUTION

13

JIM WOLFENSOHN INTRODUCED HIS VISION FOR THE ROLE OF KNOWLEDGE IN development during the 1996 Annual Meetings. He called for strategic partnerships that would take the Bank into the new millennium, creating and sharing knowledge, and making knowledge a major driver of development. Wolfensohn's vision was born out of the revolution in information technology—a revolution offering the potential to vastly extend the ability of companies to share lessons and experience with their clients in ways not possible before. He saw a great opportunity for the World Bank to tap into the knowledge of its large network of development practitioners, helping them enhance their capacity through improved access to knowledge and ideas from around the world.

The World Bank had been in the business of creating, sharing, and applying knowledge as an important part of its programs to help its member countries promote growth and reduce poverty. But only since the mid-1990s has the Bank attempted to organize its knowledge activities systematically.

Following the seminal 1996 address, Wolfensohn pushed to make sure the Bank improved its own understanding of the role of knowledge in development.

Knowledge for development

The *World Development Report 1998/1999* elevated knowledge and its application as key sources of growth in the global economy. The report argued that the increasing importance of knowledge had created both challenges and opportunities for developing countries. On the challenges, it was clear that to be competitive internationally, countries must participate effectively in the knowledge-driven supply chains and markets that now dominate the

1996

The Knowledge Bank

Wolfensohn declares during his Annual Meetings address that the World Bank will be a knowledge organization, a premier resource of knowledge for development.

WorldLinks Launched

Uganda becomes the first country to participate in WorldLinks, a joint collaboration between the World Bank and the nonprofit World Links Organization to encourage school-to-school project collaboration and serve as an information channel for teachers around the world.

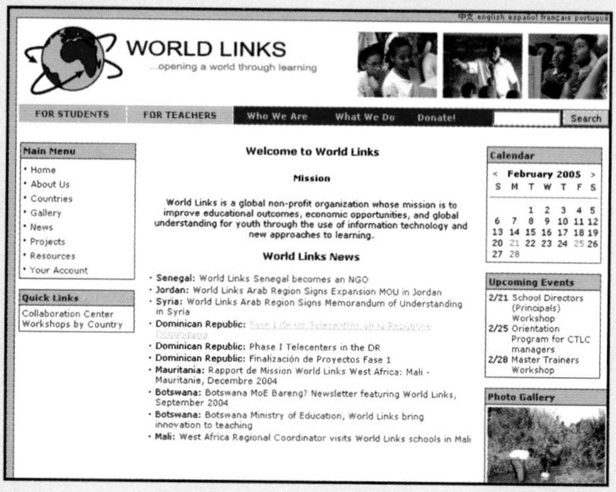

global economy. On the opportunities, it was clear that the Bank needed to help countries understand and cope with the challenges of reducing poverty and promoting sustainable development while also helping shape their futures in the knowledge economy.

To assist countries in understanding and dealing with the challenges, the Bank developed a diagnostic and policy formulation tool as part of the Knowledge for Development Program. Now the centerpiece of the World Bank's support to clients in the area of knowledge, the program helps build countries' capacity to acquire and use knowledge to strengthen their competitiveness and increase their economic and social well-being.

The program works with clients to develop realistic and achievable knowledge strategies, helping countries assess how they compare with others in their ability to compete in the knowledge economy and to identify appropriate policies to help them achieve their goals. To facilitate this process, it developed a framework consisting of four basic pillars: the economic incentive regime, education, innovation systems, and information infrastructure. To help clients self-diagnose, the program also developed a knowledge assessment methodology consisting of 80 structural and qualitative variables that serve as proxies for the four pillars.

Clients can use this assessment tool online and create their own custom diagnoses. The World Bank then supports them as they think through solutions and helps them find the opportunities to learn from others.

This approach to making the *World Development Report* on knowledge operational was a key aspect of the strategy for a "Knowledge Bank." Further thinking on the operational implications was the second main issue that Wolfensohn tackled. Leading the dialogue with various members of the

Development knowledge is part of the global commons: it belongs to everyone, and everyone should benefit from it. But a global partnership is required to cultivate and disseminate it. The Bank Group's relationships with governments and institutions all over the world, and our unique reservoir of development experience across sectors and countries, position us to play a leading role in this new global knowledge partnership.

James D. Wolfensohn,
Washington, D.C.
October 1, 1996

1997

Bringing Knowledge Together

The World Bank organizes the first Global Knowledge Conference, attended by stakeholder participants from 144 countries, leading to the formation of the Global Knowledge Partnership.

Network for Knowledge

In his Annual Meetings address, Wolfensohn states, "My goal is to make the World Bank the first port of call when people need knowledge about development. By the year 2000 we will have in place a global communications system with computer links, videoconferencing, and interactive classrooms, affording our clients all around the world full access to our information bases."

World Bank Group, he pressed for an operational strategy on knowledge, around three key dimensions.

Once the Bank had improved its understanding of the issue, the first dimension was to make effective use of knowledge to support the quality of its operations. There is a story that Wolfensohn tells about this challenge. When he first came, he would interview Bank staff to learn from them and get a sense of how well the many structural and operational reforms were working. He was stunned when he talked to a staff member retiring from the Bank, who said he was taking all his files with him to store in his garage, because he did not trust that the information would be used and saved appropriately. Wolfensohn suggested that he was stealing World Bank information and that he should leave it behind. The staff member was adamant in refusing to do so. That was when Wolfensohn discovered that there was no structured manner in which staff collected and shared critical information about the operations of the World Bank, and moreover, none to collect and leverage the tacit knowledge that staff developed over time.

Armed with this story, he pushed for tackling the issue. The Bank would establish Knowledge Communities and Advisory Services, charged with capturing the information the Bank and other institutions acquired in their areas of specialty—and processing it into useful knowledge that teams could then use.

A second critical dimension for the World Bank was sharing knowledge with clients and partners. During the early thinking about the Knowledge Bank, Wolfensohn also conceived of an approach to development, the Comprehensive Development Framework and its operational twin, the

1997
A Virtual University
The World Bank launches the African Virtual University to build capacity and support economic development by leveraging the power of modern telecommunications technology to provide world-class education and training programs to students and professionals in Africa.

1998
Knowledge Tops the Agenda
The *World Development Report 1998/1999: Knowledge for Development* proposes to look at development in a new way—from the perspective of knowledge.

DevForum Launched
DevForum is launched to promote and stimulate public debate, multidirectional knowledge sharing, and learning on key development issues and challenges facing the development community and the world's poor people.

Poverty Reduction Strategy Paper. This framework required a new way of working, making sure that client knowledge and the ideas from development partners were easily available and that the Bank could learn from them as well. Increasingly, the Bank would complement these approaches with a range of new technology-based programs that would greatly enhance its knowledge-sharing capacity.

The third dimension of operationalizing knowledge was defined around helping clients enhance their capacity to generate, tap, and use knowledge from all sources. Early work on the Comprehensive Development Framework and Poverty Reduction Strategy Papers indicated that the success of national development efforts would depend on the trained human resources and institutional arrangements available to carry them out. Supporting countries to enhance their development capacity was therefore central to the Bank's mission of poverty reduction.

Quick implementation and early wins

Ensuring that these three dimensions of knowledge were operationalized within a timeframe for testing and ensuring early successes required quick action. Within five years, the Bank put in place infrastructure and programs aimed at sharing knowledge within the organization, and increasingly with client and partners:

- Thematic communities of practice (about 100) facilitate the creation, sharing, and dissemination of experiences across internal and external boundaries. Staff could now get ideas from each other quickly, speeding the process of getting good ideas to the client. There is an example of a staff member in Senegal who, by the next morning's meeting with

1999
A Global Network of Development Knowledge
The World Bank launches the Global Development Network to support the generation and sharing of knowledge for development.

2000
A Marketplace of Ideas
The World Bank sponsors the first Development Marketplace to identify and directly support innovative bottom-up development ideas that deliver results, which can then be expanded or replicated, growing into an annual global forum with country-level marketplaces in nine countries around the globe.

the minister, needed information on the latest approach to large contracts in transport procurement. The staff member sent an e-mail out to the Transport Community of Practice, and within hours he had responses from Argentina, Pakistan, and Russia. By the next morning, he had a well-articulated report to share with the client—using information from his colleagues in the transport sector.

- Advisory services—in the form of help desks and other support services—provide quick and easy access to information, knowledge, and solutions. Among the best-known services is Rapid Response, which charges fees for services to private companies and provides free services to Bank staff.
- Regional and country programs provide customized information and knowledge services and products. The work of the Africa Region on indigenous knowledge has generated ideas for designing programs such as the HIV/AIDS strategy for Tanzania, which now builds on indigenous forms of treatment and care based on the work of an NGO in the Tanga region.
- Programs are under way to develop the skills of people in client countries to create, share, and apply knowledge. The World Bank Institute has 170 online courses or Web components of blended courses, many of them open to the public. The most dynamic of these courses is one that brings in young people from around the world to talk to CEOs of multinational corporations on the kind of future they would like to see, generating ideas on how to tackle the issue of corporate social responsibility.
- Other facilities bring together—online and face-to-face—leading development practitioners to exchange experiences and innovations. For

2000
Global Distance Learning Network Launched
Initially, a partnership of 11 learning centers, the GDLN has grown into a worldwide cooperation of more than 70 affiliates in more than 50 countries. Using advanced information and communication technologies, these learning centers now reach out virtually to every country in the world and help development practitioners connect.

2001
WorldLinks Goes Global
More than 200 schools in 10 African countries participate in WorldLinks.

example, since 1998 more than 100 e-discussions involving more than 100,000 participants have taken place on DevForum, the Bank's online discussion platform.

By 2001 the World Bank Group ranked fourth in the Most Admired Knowledge Enterprise awards, which recognize organizations for their world-class efforts in managing knowledge, leading to superior performance. Others on the list included General Electric (first), Hewlett-Packard (second), Buckman Laboratories (third), Microsoft (fifth), BP Amoco (sixth), and Siemens (seventh). The Bank Group ranked as a leading organization in four of the eight individual knowledge performance dimensions. The only public sector institution on the list, the Bank remains in the top 20.

Some major developments:

- In 1999 the Global Development Network, comprising research and policy institutes working together to address the problems of national and regional development, was launched with support from the World Bank's Development Grant Facility. Since its launch, the network has supported and linked policy research institutes from 11 regions and more than 100 countries.
- In June 2000 the Global Development Learning Network was launched to support structured and unstructured dialogue among clients. Initially a partnership of 11 learning centers, it has grown into a worldwide cooperation of more than 70 affiliates in more than 50 countries.
- In July 2001 the Development Gateway was launched to provide access to knowledge for development. Now managed by the Development Gateway Foundation, an independent not-for-profit organization, it builds partnerships and information systems and manages a very large

2001

Development Gateway Launched

Subsequently spun off from the Bank and now managed by the independent Development Gateway Foundation, the Development Gateway builds partnerships and information systems to provide access to knowledge for development.

2002

Lifelong Learning

At the Lifelong Learning Summit in Stuttgart, the World Bank releases *Constructing Knowledge Societies: New Challenges for Tertiary Education*, stating that developing countries will need to close the divide in knowledge and education in order to boost growth and reduce poverty.

database on more than 100,000 activities of the major international development donors and some civil society organizations and private foundations.

- WorldLinks helps bring the developing world into the information age through its future leaders—students. The program has expanded to more than 20 developing countries, with 200,000 students and teachers in these countries collaborating over the Internet with partners in 22 industrialized countries on projects in all disciplines.
- The African Virtual University, a network of 33 partner institutions in 18 African countries, delivers degree and diploma programs and focuses simultaneously on research and development of its technology-delivery model. The World Bank is also working in partnership with African scientists to develop the African Institutes of Science and Technology.
- The World Bank's Development Marketplace identifies and supports successful innovative bottom-up development ideas, which can then be expanded or replicated.

B-SPAN, an Internet-based broadcasting initiative, provides regular broadcasts of World Bank events through webcasts over the Internet. The Bank hosts seminars, workshops, and conferences at its Washington, D.C., headquarters where some of the world's leading development experts and practitioners discuss the latest developments in a range of sectors. The Shanghai Global Learning Process, which culminated in an international conference in May 2004, was an experiment in putting good ideas to the test by bringing in practitioners from around the world, in a nine-month-long learning program, to share ideas on what worked, what didn't, and why in reducing poverty at scale.

2004

Lessons of Shanghai

The Shanghai Global Learning Program brings together practitioners from around the world, in a nine-month-long learning program, to share ideas on "what worked, what didn't, and why" in reaching poverty reduction at scale.

The WBI has been very innovative in its efforts to spur the knowledge revolution in developing countries and to be a global catalyst for creating, sharing, and applying the cutting-edge knowledge necessary for poverty reduction and economic development. For instance, the Shanghai conference in May 2004 drew on more than 100 case studies from around the world, field visits to successful project sites, and multicountry videoconference discussions to identify what works, what doesn't, and why in scaling up poverty reduction. These lessons were shared with 250,000 people through Web sites, 15 to 20 million through print media, and about 1.6 billion through television documentaries.

14

Lending in support of country growth and poverty reduction programs is at the heart of what the Bank does. World Bank annual lending commitments averaged more than $20 billion in the early to mid-1990s, peaked at close to $29 billion in 1999 during the Asian financial crisis, and then dropped back to a steady $20 billion a year. Development policy lending (formerly known as adjustment lending) now accounts for 25 to 30 percent of total lending commitments.

Lending composition

Under Jim Wolfensohn's leadership the Bank's capacity to respond to specific development challenges was consistently established. For example, in fiscal 1998 and 1999 it doubled its lending to the countries of East Asia to help them meet the challenges of the financial crisis. To directly address the needs of poor people, it has increased its overall lending in the social sectors by more than 25 percent since 1995, to $4.7 billion annually. To revitalize the Bank Group's support for infrastructure service delivery, the Bank adopted its Infrastructure Action Plan in 2003 to provide guidance on the roles of the public and private sectors, increase infrastructure lending and policy advice, and work with other development partners to develop common approaches. IDA's commitments have increased over the past decade, from $5.7 billion in fiscal 1995 to more than $9 billion in fiscal 2004—with about half that going to African countries since 2000.

Bank lending quality

When Wolfensohn arrived the Bank tended to measure its operational performance primarily by lending commitments—numbers of dollars lent and

1996
Quality Assurance Group
Reflecting a concern with the quality of operations, the World Bank establishes the Quality Assurance Group to increase accountability by conducting real-time assessments of the quality of the Bank's performance.

1997
Introduction of Flexible Instruments
The World Bank introduces two new investment lending instruments: Adaptable Program Loans to support long-term development strategies and programs through a series of investment operations, each building on the achievements and experiences of the previous one, and Learning and Innovation Loans to "permit piloting and innovation over a relatively short time frame" and on a limited scale.

numbers of projects approved. In the early 1990s, however, both the Wapenhans Report and assessments by the Bank's independent Operational Evaluation Department (OED) identified problems with the quality of the operations the Bank was funding—according to OED, no more than about two-thirds were satisfactory or better. So in 1996, the Bank added a new dimension to its indicators of operational performance—quality—and created a program to improve operational quality. The major element in that program was management's constant, unflagging attention to the issue, supported by a newly created Quality Assurance Group. The outcome of the program was a remarkable recovery in quality. By fiscal 2000 the proportion of operations that reached satisfactory outcomes stood at 76 percent, a full 20 percentage points above the lowest results a few years earlier.

Paradigm shift

The operational-quality improvement coincided with an important shift in the way the Bank thought about its work—from a project perspective to a country perspective. Wolfensohn has always emphasized the need for countries to "own" their development process, instead of having priorities and projects pushed on them by well-meaning donors. With the country "in the driver's seat," as Wolfensohn expressed it, there is a greater sense of partnership between country clients and the Bank.

Today, the Bank encourages countries to articulate their own development priorities and strategies and to decide how they want the Bank and other donors to support those priorities. Increasingly, Bank assistance is based on the country's objectives, taking into account the overall policy environment, analytical work on the constraints to development in the country, and

1999
Comprehensive Development Framework
Wolfensohn articulates the Comprehensive Development Framework.

2001
Transparency in Operations
The World Bank Board adopts a new disclosure policy.

the work of other development partners. This evolution is reflected in the Bank's approach to country programming. In the late 1980s it involved simple internal summaries of projects for each country. Today it includes results-based country assistance strategies discussed with the client government, country stakeholders, and development partners, and made public after review by the Bank's Executive Directors.

Instrument mix

The Bank offers a range of instruments to meet each country's development needs. As a bank, it offers various kinds of loans for a variety of purposes, from small technical assistance projects to large financial sector reform programs. And for these loans it has several sets of financial terms determined by country circumstances. The Bank also offers grant programs, providing funds that recipients do not need to pay back. In addition, it offers a broad set of analytical and advisory services—diagnostic studies, technical assistance, and just-in-time policy advice. The Bank's country assistance strategy usually includes a mix of these instruments that the Bank and borrower agree will provide the most appropriate way for the Bank to support the country in achieving its development priorities.

Participation

Wolfensohn understood that full country ownership of a development program or project means more than just agreement by a finance minister—it requires broad understanding and backing by the entire government, and by the population as well. He set a good example by meeting with a wide range of people—representatives of the private sector, nongovernmental

2002
Modernization and Simplification
Operations Policy and Country Services launches its initiative to modernize and simplify Bank policies, procedures, processes, and products.

2003
Harmonization
At the Rome High-Level Forum on Harmonization, the Bank joins other participants in deepening the concept of harmonization, encouraging country ownership, and focusing on implementation at the country level.

organizations, and faith-based groups—and he encouraged the development of a culture of participation in the Bank's operations. The Bank now routinely includes consultations in all facets of its work—country assistance strategy development, project preparation, monitoring and evaluation, and the development of its own policies. It also expects borrowing countries to increasingly ensure that their interactions with the Bank involve public participation.

Financing from the World Bank has been and continues to be extremely important for the government's activity. For example, the restructuring of the coal industry, on which over $1 billion was spent. Or social projects in municipal formations and large cities of the Russian Federation. Or medical projects in a number of Russian cities.

Vladimir Putin
President of Russia

Instrument update

After Wolfensohn joined the Bank it became clear that the Bank's policies and procedures were not keeping pace with the evolution of the development paradigm. In the early years of the 21st century the Bank realized that its lending—the backbone of its development work—was declining. It learned that its rigid policy framework was a major reason. Some policies were outdated, hard to understand, and at times contradictory. Moreover, procedures were cumbersome and slow. Bank staff complained about the difficulty of meeting borrower needs under these circumstances. Borrowers, in turn, complained about the high costs and administrative hurdles in obtaining and using Bank finance.

Simplification and modernization

Wolfensohn understood that if the Bank was to be responsive to clients, it would have to address these problems more effectively. So, he supported a comprehensive program to reform—to simplify and modernize—the Bank's lending, credit, and grant instruments, while maintaining the quality of the Bank's work. The reform had five objectives:

Streamlined Project Preparation

Streamlined templates are introduced for the new Project Concept Note and Project Appraisal Document, and streamlined procedures are introduced for simple and repeater projects—reducing average preparation time from 18 months to 14 months.

2004

Managing for Results

At the Second International Roundtable on Managing for Development Results in Marrakech, the World Bank joins other participants in deepening the global partnership on managing for results.

- To develop a clear, coherent, and user-friendly policy framework for lending.
- To modernize the Bank's lending instruments to allow more flexible responses to client demands and varying country circumstances.
- To enable faster processing of operations through simplified procedures, clearer guidelines, and improved documentation.
- To put greater emphasis on strengthening countries' own systems and institutions and building country capacities.
- To promote more effective implementation of Bank-financed operations and to achieve stronger development results.

This sweeping agenda required action on several fronts at once.

Modernized development policy instrument

One of the most significant steps in the reform program was a rethinking of nonproject lending to underline the point that this instrument can most effectively support a country in reforming its policy framework. Since this lending was introduced at the beginning of the 1980s, it had been called adjustment lending—with the implication that it was designed to fix what was wrong with the borrowing country. Under the Bank's operational reform program, it was renamed development policy lending to reflect its support of governments' efforts to meet the needs of their countries. The instrument's approach also changed with its name: it now emphasizes country ownership of the reform program, embraces consultation with and participation of stakeholders, and requires greater systematic attention to the possible effects of policy changes on society, poverty, and the environment.

Eligibility for Financing
The World Bank introduces expanded eligibility for financing, more closely aligning what the Bank can finance with what borrowers need to spend to successfully implement projects and programs.

From Adjustment to Development Policy Lending
The Bank replaces its adjustment lending instrument with a development policy lending instrument that emphasizes country ownership, participation, and results.

Modernization of the investment instrument

The Bank is also reforming its tools for investment lending—the type of lending that finances specific investment projects—to increase its development impact. Over the past decades the Bank had developed a wide range of specific instruments for investment lending, but it has concluded that a major streamlining is needed. It is examining how to increase the effectiveness of "adaptable" lending—lending that allows for scaling up a project through a phased approach. It is improving its ability to provide additional financing to projects when that makes sense. And it is assessing whether it has flexible enough instruments to address the needs of borrowers stricken by various types of crises or emergencies.

Policy framework

Bank investment lending is governed by more than 30 complex policy statements, a situation that works against expeditious, transparent processing. The Bank is thus working to rationalize its suite of policies. In the meantime, it has changed some of its policies to support the new ways of doing business. For example, it has updated the policy on expenditure eligibility to make it easier for the Bank to finance a broad array of the expenditures that borrowers need to make to implement agreed projects. It has updated its procurement policies and is working on its disbursement policies. It has also clarified its policy on participation in pooled financing to support sectorwide approaches. And it has streamlined its approach to project auditing.

Faster processing

The Bank introduced changes in its documents and procedures that would allow projects to be processed more quickly, so that the borrower would

2005

Supervision Reporting

The World Bank replaces the Project Status Report with the Implementation Status and Results Report to strengthen project management and results reporting.

Using Country Systems

The Bank launches a pilot program to test the use of a country's own environmental and social systems in Bank-financed operations, facilitating a focus on supporting the development and application of effective policies for all government spending.

receive funds and be able to address an identified need more promptly and benefit from the project's results sooner. Project documents were simplified to enable staff to present projects for Board approval in a shorter time. Procedures for some types of projects—such as simpler projects and repeater projects—were streamlined. And line-management responsibilities for review and clearance were clarified. Overall, these changes helped reduce average project processing time from 18 months to 14 months.

Ongoing process

As a result of all these changes, the Bank has evolved in ways that consistently reflect Wolfensohn's emphasis on responsiveness to clients. It can respond more flexibly to countries' unique needs and to situations that may arise while projects are being implemented. It can scale up successful approaches for greater development results and process projects more quickly. And it is making good progress with reforms to its policy framework to make its policies and procedures clearer, more coherent, and comprehensive. The Bank recognizes, however, that reform is likely to be an ongoing process. It expects to continue to review and refine its policies, procedures, and instruments to meet its borrowers' changing development needs.

Alignment with country systems

Concurrently, the development community was coming to the realization that its traditional way of delivering assistance—through project implementation units separate from borrowers' governments—was undermining, rather than building, countries' capacity to be responsible for their own development programs. The evolving understanding was that countries

2005

Harmonization, Alignment, and Results

The World Bank leads the organization of the Paris High-Level Forum on Harmonization, Alignment, and Results, which strengthens the link between harmonization and results and identifies a specific list of indicators to track harmonization progress by countries and development partners.

Additional Finance

The Executive Directors consider a modified policy that makes it easier, faster, and cheaper to scale up successful projects.

would be able to build and improve their internal systems only by using them, rather than having many separate systems prescribed from outside by multiple donors.

The World Bank and other development agencies began to work on ways to depend more on borrowing-country systems: reducing the numbers of project implementation units, establishing various innovative arrangements for capacity building, and experimenting with selective use of country systems for financial management, procurement, and environmental assessment in certain countries, sectors, and projects.

In early 2005 the World Bank launched a pilot program to test issues surrounding this kind of change. It will regularly report its findings as the program evolves. This area is so integral to the future of development, and has so many different facets, that it appears likely to be one of the main challenges for the development community in the next few years.

2005
The Bank launches a pilot program to test the greater use of borrowing-country systems.

15

THE INTERNATIONAL BANK FOR RECONSTRUCTION AND DEVELOPMENT (IBRD) and the International Development Association (IDA) are commonly called the "World Bank." IBRD—operating similar to a bank that raises funds in international capital markets—aims to reduce poverty in middle-income and creditworthy poorer countries by promoting sustainable development through loans, guarantees, and (nonlending) analytical and advisory services. IDA provides interest-free credit and grants to countries that have little or no capacity to borrow on market terms.

Over the last decade the IBRD has launched new lending products, introduced a broader range of financial services, upgraded electronic and procedural systems, strengthened the financial management cadres, created state-of-the art governance principles and controls, developed sophisticated risk metrics, and strengthened the financial fundamentals. In short, the IBRD has been better positioned financially to contribute to the unfinished agenda of poverty alleviation.

Financial health and modern risk management

The last decade saw substantial improvement in the financial health of the IBRD's balance sheet, a result of modern risk-management techniques and best-practice systems for assessing and managing the Bank's capital adequacy. This has resulted in a $6 billion increase in usable equity and a substantial improvement in the IBRD's equity-loan ratio.

The key to modern risk management was the Risk-Adjusted Allocation of Capital (RAAC) framework. In keeping with best practice in the financial services industry, the RAAC was introduced in fiscal 1998 as a comprehensive portfolio risk model able to summarize the various factors

1995
Stronger Internal Controls
The Bank adopts the Committee of Sponsoring Organizations of the Treadway Commission–based integrated internal control framework to evaluate the effectiveness of its internal control system.

1996
More Choices for Clients
The IBRD introduces the variable spread loan to offer a one-time choice of currency and interest rate basis on loans, and the fixed-rate single currency loan, as well as the opportunity to convert existing currency pool loans to the offered currency of choice.

that drive credit risk within IBRD's loan portfolio into one simple risk metric. In developing the RAAC, the IBRD had to adapt concepts used by leading commercial banks to its unique business environment. Before this the IBRD, like other multilateral investment banks, had used various simple income and balance-sheet-related ratios to gauge the adequacy of its capital.

Building on the ability conferred by the RAAC model, the IBRD developed a more sophisticated "stress test" methodology for assessing its capital adequacy in fiscal 1999. Under the new methodology, the adequacy of IBRD's capital was assessed as what would ensure that the IBRD would continue to have sufficient financial capacity to absorb certain types of income losses and still generate sufficient income, with waivers and transfers pulled, to support loan growth while allowing a gradual recovery of its post-shock equity-loan ratio.

Partly as a result, the IBRD's usable equity capital increased by more than $6 billion between fiscal 1995 and fiscal 2005, while the Bank's equity-loan ratio has increased from about 20 percent then to about 30 percent now. This is an unambiguous statement about the health of the Bank's balance sheet.

New financial products

As a financial cooperative, the World Bank is interested in all aspects of its member countries' financial capacity. In line with this comprehensive outlook, the role of the IBRD with its clients has evolved from a provider of development assistance to a financial partner, delivering lending services in a financing package. Along with new financial products, the IBRD now

1997

Modernizing Risk Management

The Bank strengthens management of its credit risk within its loan portfolio with the Risk-Adjusted Allocation of Capital (RAAC) framework.

1998

Stress Test

The Bank develops a more sophisticated methodology to assess the IBRD's capital adequacy to ensure its continuing capacity to weather certain types of losses and preserve income, resulting in a $6 billion increase in usable equity capital and an equity-loan ratio increase from 20 percent to 30 percent.

Strengthened Reporting

The Bank begins to develop a robust hierarchy of analytical financial reports that puts it in the vanguard of international organizations in financial reporting.

Investing in Staff

The Bank undertakes an institutional initiative to rebuild the cadre of financial management specialists in the Regions from approimately 25 in the late 1990s to some 125 in 2005. This is done to strengthen the Bank's fiduciary assurance over lending.

provides market-based instruments to help clients manage their financial risks. Other multilateral development banks have emulated the IBRD's shift away from pool-based products to more market-based financial products.

The evolution of the IBRD's financial products has mirrored that of capital markets over the past two decades—and matched its clients' increasing financial sophistication. When Jim Wolfensohn took over, clients had access to only a single kind of loan instrument—with no choice of currency—priced on the basis of an underlying currency pool, hence the title currency pool loan (CPL). Bank clients were exposed to financial risk to the extent that the CPL currency and interest-rate basis were not appropriate for their risk management needs. To match developments in financial markets, the IBRD announced two initiatives in 1996 to broaden the choices available to clients: a one-time choice of currency and interest-rate basis at inception through the variable spread loan, which had an interest rate based on LIBOR (the London interbank offered rate), the fixed-rate single currency loan, and the ability to convert the terms of their existing CPLs to the offered currency of their choice.

Wolfensohn announced, "We should use our tremendous intermediation capacity to mobilize financing for projects and programs on the range of terms and currencies requested by borrowers. We appreciate the funding access our major developed-country shareholders are providing to enable us to take this step and look forward to continuing to broaden our financial product and services menu to meet our clients' needs."

In 1999 the IBRD retired the CPL and, in a move that transformed both how the IBRD does business and the capacity of developing countries to access derivatives markets, it made the world of hedges available to its clients

1999

Bringing Flexibility to Clients

The Bank retires the currency pool loan and introduces fixed spread loans. It also introduces hedging and derivatives as options for its clients through a range of new product offerings—all accompanied by a massive outreach.

Integrated Accounting Systems

The Bank's disparate legacy controllers and corporate accounting systems are replaced by SAP, a state-of-the-art enterprise resource management system, providing an integrated and globally deployable system with improved reporting capability that fosters business renewal.

to use in conjunction with their IBRD loans. Although the financial instruments commonly used to manage currency and interest-rate risk have been used since the 1980s—derivatives such as currency and interest-rate swaps—IBRD clients' credit ratings have typically limited their access to these instruments. By intermediating for its clients through the use of its highly rated balance sheet, the IBRD is filling a need that the private sector is currently unable to meet.

The fixed spread loan features a LIBOR-based interest rate and includes options to convert the currency and interest rate, or cap/collar the interest rate, and features greater flexibility to tailor the repayment schedule, with maturities in some cases of up to 25 years. Freestanding hedging products allow IBRD clients to conduct a full range of hedging activities to mitigate the risk associated with older IBRD loans, including variable spread loans, fixed-rate single currency loans, and CPLs. Currency swaps, interest-rate swaps, interest-rate caps and collars, and commodity swaps were also introduced.

In December 2000 the IBRD introduced local currency financing products in response to borrowers' desire to reduce their currency risk exposure at the sovereign or subsovereign level, because many borrowers' principal revenue streams are in local currency.

The IBRD's financial products have received strong endorsements from borrowers. The fixed spread loan now makes up about two-thirds of new loan commitments.

Better controls and reporting

The Bank has also radically transformed its control functions. Once seen as a relative backwater with a primary focus on transaction processing and

2000

Reducing Currency Risk Exposure for Clients

The Bank introduces local currency financing products for the first time.

2001

Lower Cost, Stronger Controls

A significant portion of the Bank's accounting services are offshored to Chennai, India, enabling the Bank to reduce the cost of processing and focus on strengthening controls.

minimalist reporting, these functions now match the standards of worldwide best practice and have credibility and influence both within the organization and with global players in the arena of international accounting and auditing architecture.

Before 1998 financial reporting was somewhat sparse, providing only basic financial data. Since that time, a more robust hierarchy of analytical financial reports has been developed to provide a diverse array of readers—the Board, management, rating agencies, underwriters, and other interested parties—information relevant to their needs.

The complexity and depth of the Bank's financial statements have increased significantly, and they are now accompanied by a management discussion and analysis that communicates the Bank's financial structure, governance, and results in detail. The Bank has also been in the vanguard of organizations reporting under international financial reporting standards for many years and has kept pace with the recent unprecedented volume and velocity of new reporting requirements, concurrently dealing with a range of underlying Bank transactions, which have become significantly more complex—particularly in Treasury with the extensive use of derivatives and the development of new, more flexible loan products.

Though not formally required to comply with U.S. legislation, the Bank also adopted in 2004 many of the requirements of the U.S. Sarbanes-Oxley Act ahead of other organizations, in recognition of the recent global evolution of corporate governance and internal control best practices. In so doing, the Bank is at the forefront of best practice in relation to major U.S. corporations.

2003
Client Connection
The Bank launches an online service to provide clients with access to portfolio information and knowledge repositories.

In 2003 the Bank launched Client Connection, a secure Internet site that enables registered users to access confidential country, project, and financial information in real time, as well as a wealth of public information to support informed business decisions.

Going forward

The Bank will continue to build on this foundation. Going forward, a key part of the unfinished agenda will be the ongoing efforts at budget reform.

2004

Ahead of the Curve

Though not required to do so, the Bank adopts many requirements of U.S. Sarbanes-Oxley legislation enacted in response to corporate scandals, placing the Bank at the forefront of best practice in relation to major corporations based in the United States.

16

IN EARLY 1995 THE WORLD BANK WAS IN A TAILSPIN. EMBARRASSED BOTH BY internal missteps and by sometimes-misguided external interests, it had not only lost its focus—it had lost its sense of being. Morale was low, and staff were more cynical than ever. People talked openly of the Bank's decline, the budget restrictions, and the further reductions of staff and resources to perform an already difficult job.

Jim Wolfensohn, as a leading investment banker and chairman of the Kennedy Center and Carnegie Hall, was a surprise to the typically low-key institution. Its professional staff wondered out loud about the impact of such an appointment on their careers and fortunes. In April 1995 the Bank's annual internal satirical magazine, "Bank Swirled," commenting on the possibility of layoffs, wrote: "James D. Wolfensohn, Inc. manages a portfolio of over $10 billion in investments with 150 staff worldwide. Our lending was $20 billion last year, and we have over 8,000 staff on board. What do you think?"

The coming 10 years would prove far different from what anyone had contemplated.

Amid the cynicism was a distinct new energy. Wolfensohn was committed to development. And his style, even before he officially took the helm of the Bank in June 1995, provided hints of how he wanted to run the business. He moved into a suite of offices early in April, two months before he officially started. He started work very early—he stayed late into the night. He ate in the Bank's cafeteria or carried his lunch in a brown paper bag. Wherever he went in the Bank, he spoke to staff, engaged them for opinions (formally as well as informally), and greeted them warmly—a far different style from past presidents. His IDEAS Line gave staff a direct

1995
10,283 World Bank Staff, 17 Percent in Country Offices

Staff Exchanges
The World Bank begins exchanging staff with other organizations to facilitate knowledge sharing across the global development community.

1996
Rewarding Excellence
The President's Award for Excellence is introduced to recognize outstanding contributions by staff.

Decentralization and Networks
Reorganization brings the formation of networks and the first country directors located in the field.

connection to his office. And he insisted on excellence from everyone around him—reinforcing that insistence by demanding even more from himself.

The impact on the human resources front was immediate and deep reaching. As he said in his first address to the Bank, "I want us to be the experts. I want to ensure that our staff are the best because what we do for our clients demands the best."

Technical excellence

Human resource reforms were already under way as Wolfensohn assumed the presidency. But they took on a new life as his management style began to emerge.

By 1996 Wolfensohn had asked enough questions and had come to some firm conclusions. The Bank needed to demonstrate global technical excellence—its "comparative value" when judged against regional lenders. It needed to be more client-facing and much more responsive to their needs. And it needed to stop working in isolation and reach out through teamwork and partnerships.

The cultural shift in the Bank began with "the matrix" and the first of the networks in 1996. In creating the Human Development Network as a pilot for the initiative, Wolfensohn sought to merge the human assets, the "human capital," of an institution traditionally divided into small, isolated units and between subject-matter experts and practitioners, and to concentrate both on the overall needs of clients—alleviating poverty.

By 1998 "Wolfensohn's Bank" could point to more than 100 communities of practice in six distinct networks. Technical excellence was a matter of

People lie at the heart of the Bank's renewal. Our success or failure will depend on the quality of our staff. In the Strategic Compact, we promised a thorough review of the Bank's human resources policy. . . Central to the new framework is a recognition that we need to attract and retain the best people from all over the world, treat them fairly over the course of their Bank careers, and foster teamwork, learning, and innovation across the institution.

James D. Wolfensohn
March 5, 1998

1997
EDP Launched
The Executive Development Program provides Bank managers with the opportunity to learn new skills, strengthen core knowledge, and enhance managerial effectiveness.

1998
Staff Equity
The inequitable situation of nonregular staff begins to be phased out.

Decentralization has enabled our programs to grow in knowledge, reach, and relevance, with better and more tailormade strategies to guide our own poverty reduction strategies. It has also enabled us to build much closer working relationships not only with government counterparts but also with donors, the private sector, and broader civil society.

Ian Porter
Country Director
World Bank

peer review and feedback from the networks. And the Bank's global expertise was being applied region by region through its networks.

Managerial excellence

The matrix structure resulted in 200 new managerial positions—country and sector directors. This was Wolfensohn's opportunity to rebuild the Bank's management culture. Despite unease from the Bank's Board and staff, Wolfensohn held steadfast: each position would be open to competition from both within and outside the Bank. In a span of two months, several hundred managers underwent the scrutiny of a revamped managerial selection process, still operating today, based on leadership behavior and results. The objective was twofold: to signal the reality of the Bank's changing culture to both itself and its clients, and to demonstrate that transparency and results were part of that new culture.

The focus on managerial excellence has since been expanded to include the notion of management as a "corporate asset," deployed through strategic reassignments in response to business needs. Each year, up to 30 percent of managerial positions are now handled through reassignments, 70 percent through competitive selection.

In parallel, Wolfensohn's belief that effectiveness is best judged through multiple perspectives resulted in the introduction of a 360-degree feedback mechanism. Managers would now hear not only from their bosses, but also from their clients, peers, and subordinates. Performance and "fit" issues would be addressed swiftly: when personal coaching and learning did not work, managers were removed from their position—an approach that has yielded a 20 percent turnover in managerial ranks over the past few years.

1999
Aligning Compensation with the Market
The Bank emphasizes a market-based compensation system, including for country offices.

2000
Building Staff Knowledge
The World Bank appoints its first chief learning officer and forms a Learning Board to strengthen professional development of staff.

To strengthen the Bank's connection to the realities of the rest of the world, Wolfensohn launched an Executive Development Program in partnership with the business schools of Harvard, Stanford, France's INSEAD, Spain's IESE, and the Kennedy School of Government—providing the Bank's "best and brightest" with the opportunity to learn new skills, strengthen core knowledge, and enhance managerial effectiveness. The truly remarkable innovation was in bringing together such unlikely classmates as "old school" and "new school" staff, their government clients, and even traditional "adversaries" from NGOs to lay the foundations for a common and open dialogue—effectively creating a new breed of managers. In the program's four-year run, more than 800 managers in eight "cohorts" shared an experience that many still recount as the highlight of their careers.

Competition, equity, fairness

This notion of competition from within and outside also began to play out across all jobs within the Bank. Once again, Wolfensohn's theme of having the right people for the right jobs catalyzed new human resources policies. Today, those principles are embedded in promotion and selection criteria, requiring experience in the field or work with our poorest countries, across multiple regions, and in partnership with people across and outside the Bank.

Wolfensohn's belief that "the face we present and the voice we speak should be that of the world's bank" resulted in several key appointments: the first director for diversity, the first racial advisor, and the first advisor on disabilities. Today, the World Bank's staff better reflect the profile of its clients: nationals from developing countries now account for half the total staff, including a full 10 percent from the Sub-Saharan Africa and Latin

2001
Valuing Diversity
The Bank forms an Integrated Office of Diversity, covering gender, race, and disability.

2002
Strengthening Decentralization
The Bank adopts human resources policies to better support decentralization of staff, and strengthens benefits for country office staff to introduce greater parity for locally recruited colleagues.

Strategic Placement of Managers
The Bank inaugurates managerial strategic reassignments, recognizing managers as "corporate assets." Up to a third of all managerial posts are now filled through strategic reassignments, with the remaining filled through competitive selection.

America and Caribbean regions. Women make up more than 40 percent of staff, a quarter of them in senior positions.

In 1998 long-term contingent staff—who had been working side-by-side with core staff but with reduced benefits—were integrated into the organization. Administrative staff, unsung heroes to some, were given recognition in the form of their own network of practitioners and learning. And locally hired national staff saw expanded benefits and a sharper focus on their career paths. "Think globally, act locally" was becoming a reality.

Further reinforcing the notions of equity and fairness, Wolfensohn spearheaded a state-of-the-art conflict resolution system, opening informal and formal avenues for staff to preserve fairness in the workplace and maintain a positive working environment for everyone. The system expanded and consolidated disparate parts of a staff grievance apparatus to encompass the services of ombudsmen, mediation and ethics officers, respectful workplace advisors, and appeals and administrative tribunal offices. Mirroring his strong stance on corruption, a new Internal Investigation Unit would ensure that fraud and corruption—internal and external—and allegations of staff misconduct would be addressed promptly.

Turned to the client, responsive

With the shift in culture, human resources addressed the issue of decentralizing the Bank. If the Bank was to become more responsive to its clients' needs, it would need to be closer to its clients geographically. And being closer to its clients would require the Bank to become more accountable to them.

Human resources' response was to revamp its policies concerning its local offices. In 1996 only 17 percent of staff were located in the field.

2004

Rewarding Diversity

The Bank gives its first Diversity and Inclusion Leadership Awards to staff whose sustained efforts have contributed to meaningful change in enhancing diversity and inclusion in the World Bank working environment.

Global Mobility Center

The Bank launches this service to promote worldwide mobility of staff by providing support for spouse or partner career, education, settling in, and cross-cultural services.

Today, 73 percent of country directors live and work outside the Bank's Washington, D.C., headquarters—as do 40 to 60 percent of its technical staff—depending on the region.

The practicalities of this geographical shift resulted in new guidelines for compensation equity (based on market-based comparators). The need to support those families of staff who had been relocated was met with the creation of a Global Mobility Center. And career-growth guidelines mandated country office experience as an integral factor in promotions to higher grade levels.

Decentralization also meant a more global role for human resources. No longer Washington-bound, Wolfensohn's human resources professionals were now providing advice and counsel to Bank clients—extending the impact of his reforms beyond his own organization. Whether in the field of knowledge management or distance learning, the Bank was becoming the Knowledge Bank he had called for in 1997. And he was using human resources' inherent role in the organization to enlist hearts and recruit minds to meet the Bank's objectives.

Although it is easy to point out the operational impact of Wolfensohn's presidency on the work of the World Bank, the more significant and lasting accomplishment may be his impact on the Bank's culture. In the last 10 years, the 60-year-old institution has flattened its organizational structure—ridding itself of the excessive trappings of hierarchy and its status symbols, making communications flow more directly, and creating a sense of inclusion so that staff feel that their contributions are important and that they are part of a unique and powerful endeavor. In the 2004 Staff Survey, 92 percent of Bank staff indicated that they are "proud to work for the Bank," and 72 percent responded that they "feel valued as a staff member."

We are all team members, irrespective of whether we come from the local office, from Washington, from a nearby country office, or even a distant one, in another region. Location is no longer a predictor for competence, knowledge, and experience.

Ana Maria Sandhi
Lead Education Specialist,
Romania
World Bank

Revised Promotion and Selection Criteria
The criteria are revised to recognize the concept of global experience as the strength of Bank staff.

2005
10,728 World Bank Staff, 32 Percent in Country Offices

17

THE NEED TO BETTER MANAGE FOR RESULTS—TO USE INFORMATION TO IMPROVE decisionmaking and steer country-led development processes toward clearly defined goals—emerged at the forefront of the global development agenda in the post-Monterrey period. Jim Wolfensohn has been at the cutting edge of this issue throughout his tenure at the Bank. Indeed, the World Bank's agenda on managing for results is rooted in the mid-1990s shift to a more country-focused approach, a key theme throughout his efforts to reform the Bank.

This approach recognizes the country's development program, not the traditional project cycle, as the core business model for the Bank. It acknowledges the centrality of the country, a point Wolfensohn continually stressed, and confirms the Bank's role as a support of policy and institutional changes at the country level. Operationally, this iterative approach starts with the country's vision and agenda, applies diagnostic tools to determine the appropriate level and forms of Bank support, and uses information on progress toward results to guide future strategy and implementation.

Development partners will find it difficult to manage for results if countries are unable to do so. At its most fundamental level, the results agenda is about helping countries, as well as staffs of donor agencies, to ask themselves, "Are we being effective?" and "How do we know?" Information about results is fundamental to both learning and accountability.

Evolution of the results agenda

The Bank traditionally has had fairly strong systems to track deliveries and monitor and evaluate development outcomes at the project level, yielding reliable time-series data for learning and accountability purposes. In the

1995
Focus on Results
In his Annual Meetings address, Wolfensohn outlines a focus on excellence and results as one of four themes that will shape his agenda.

1996
Quality Agenda
The Bank embarks on a program to improve operational quality and results on the ground. The Quality Assurance Group is established.

Quality at Entry
The Quality Assurance Group launches Quality at Entry Assessments.

move to enhance development effectiveness, the Bank has undertaken extensive efforts to improve the operational quality of Bank-supported operations and analytical work and focus increasingly on results on the ground. A rising trend in satisfactory project outcomes mirrored upward trends in the quality of operational design, supervision, and analytical work in the late 1990s and early 2000s.

At the end of the day, only results in the field count.

James D. Wolfensohn
January 7, 2004

Monterrey Consensus

The May 2002 International Conference on Financing for Development in Monterrey was an important external reinforcement for the Bank's agenda on managing for results. In calling for developing countries to strengthen their commitment to policies and institutions that stimulate growth and reduce poverty, and for developed countries both to provide more—and more effective—aid and to improve their trade and debt policies, the Monterrey Consensus underscored a shared responsibility for achieving development results. A joint statement by the heads of the multilateral development banks underscored Wolfensohn's commitment to a greater focus on results. The statement highlighted the centrality of the country context; the alignment of agencies' programs with country priorities within a country-led partnership; the scaling up of efforts to improve measuring, monitoring, and managing for results; and the strengthening of country capacity for public sector management to enhance transparency and mutual accountability for development results.

The results agenda was defined in the course of 2002 as a key step in the World Bank's efforts to improve delivery, operational quality, and aid effectiveness. Implementation of the Bankwide agenda on better managing for

1997
Quality of Supervision
The Quality Assurance Group launches Quality of Supervision Assessments.

1998
Quality of Economic and Sector Work
The Quality Assurance Group mainstreams assessments of Quality of Economic and Sector Work.

results began in 2003 with an Implementation Action Plan that called for actions on three pillars:

- In countries, where development results are achieved, to strengthen both capacity and demand to manage for results.
- In the Bank, to enhance the relevance and effectiveness of our contribution to results.
- Across development agencies, to harmonize results-based approaches and better coordinate support to strengthen country capacity to manage for results.

Strengthening country demand and capacity to manage for results

Developing countries need both sustained political will and national institutional capacity to manage for results. This is the central issue of the results agenda and its most difficult challenge. To address this challenge, the Bank helps countries strengthen national strategic planning (including for poverty reduction strategies) and provides support for results-based public sector management, statistical capacity, and monitoring and evaluation systems. Initial progress includes strengthened guidance on the design, monitoring, and evaluation of Poverty Reduction Strategy Papers (PRSPs), and demand-driven support to countries for assessing their institutional readiness and strengthening results-based approaches to public sector management. An important step forward was the development of the Statistical Capacity Building Program—approved by the Board in March 2004—which provides a sectorwide approach to building capacity based on a strategic statistical plan for providing reliable and timely data on countries' core development outcomes as articulated in their PRSPs or national development strategies.

1999
Comprehensive Development Framework
Wolfensohn articulates the Comprehensive Development Framework, with its focus on results.

2000
Monitoring and Evaluation Improvement Program
The Committee on Development Effectiveness discusses recommendations from a Bankwide task force to address causes of poor monitoring and evaluation through a focused improvement program.

DEVELOPMENT STATISTICS AT THE WORLD BANK

Statistics are a public good, used by many but produced by a few. In the development field, they are needed to provide the evidence base for policy and for measuring results. Global agencies such as the World Bank, which use statistics in their work, also have an obligation to ensure that the data producers, mostly national statistical offices, receive the support and recognition they deserve. Jim Wolfensohn's presidency has given new prominence to the importance of statistics in the work of the Bank. when he first went to Africa, for example, his insistence on having a good statistical profile for the countries he was visiting led to the production of "at-a-glance" tables, now widely used throughout the Bank.

The Strategic Compact, launched at the beginning of Wolfensohn's presidency, called for monitoring important development indicators and reporting on progress through the newly redesigned *World Development Indicators* publication, launched in 1997. Subsequently, the Comprehensive Development Framework called for regular reporting on country development targets, a process that has been actively taken up in national poverty reduction strategies. In June 2000 *A Better World for All*, the first comprehensive report to measure progress toward the international development goals, was published and signed by the heads of the UN, IMF, OECD, and World Bank. Since the Millennium Summit in September 2000, the targets and indicators of the Millennium Development Goals and the increased emphasis on results have focused international attention on the problems of underdevelopment and inequality and have brought renewed urgency to the need for better data.

The increased demand for data on all aspects of development requires improvements in their supply. Under Jim Wolfensohn, institutional capacities to provide timely and reliable data for users at both national and international levels have been substantially improved. The emphasis has moved from simply compiling international indicators to addressing basic weaknesses in the source data and helping developing countries produce and use statistics more effectively.

- The Bank was instrumental in establishing the Partnership in Statistics for Development in the 21st Century (PARIS21), which works with statistics producers and users around the world to make the case for better data and to promote more effective coordination.
- The Bank's multidonor Trust Fund for Statistical Capacity Building provides seed money for launching new and innovative capacity-building projects.
- In 2004 a new multicountry lending program for statistical capacity building—STATCAP—was launched. Besides issuing the flagship *World Development Indicators* publication, now recognized as the leading source of development indicators worldwide, the Bank has been active in developing tools to help users access and use statistics from different sources.
- In 2004 the Development Data Platform (DDP) was launched as a user-friendly, Internet-based tool for data access and analysis.

By the end of Jim Wolfensohn's presidency, development statistics has been thoroughly established as a core Bank program, and the Bank is recognized as a global leader and innovator in this field. At the closing of the Second Roundtable on Managing for Development Results in Marrakech, Morocco, in February 2004, Wolfensohn said of the Marrakech Action Plans for Statistics (MAPS): "This is more than a detail. This is at the center of our ability to demonstrate progress and we have been too long in giving this the appropriate weighting."

Of course, there is still more to do. MAPS calls for further actions and investment at the country and international levels to meet the data challenges of the results management agenda and the Millennium Development Goals. Key initiatives already under way include helping all developing countries prepare and implement national strategies for developing their statistical systems, the creation of an international household survey network, and the successful completion of the latest round of the international price-comparison program.

When Jim Wolfensohn came to the Bank, he asked for good data. As he leaves, his legacy is an unprecedented opportunity for real progress and a sustainable improvement in the quality and availability of development statistics.

—*Shaida Badiee*

The Bank has also taken steps to stimulate more proactive and deliberate action among the donor community by developing a system for measuring statistical capacity at the country level. Starting in fiscal 2006, this measure will be an internal key performance indicator, signaling to staff the importance of systematically working with clients to build demand and capacity to use evidence of effectiveness in decisionmaking.

Enhancing the Bank's contribution to development results

Progress has been significant in increasing the focus on results in Bank strategies, instruments, incentives, and reporting systems. Country teams have been piloting a central element of the agenda: moving to a results-based country assistance strategy that shifts the focus to country-level results and more explicitly links these results to the choice of products and services within Bank programming. An important part of preparing a results-based country assistance strategy is the new instrument of self-evaluation—a country assistance strategy completion report—which summarizes progress under the existing country assistance strategy framework. Sector Boards have also strengthened the results frameworks and outcome monitoring for sector and thematic strategies. Revision in the contents of basic documents and Bank procedures has begun to strengthen the articulation of outcome-oriented objectives and monitoring for Bank operations. And a Results Measurement System was developed for implementation during IDA14 consisting of two tiers: tracking "big picture" outcomes on 14 outcome indicators, and focusing on IDA's contribution through the results-based country assistance strategy and in specific projects.

2001

Focus on Monitoring and Evaluation

Operations Policy and Country Services issues guidance on selecting performance indicators for Bank-supported operations and establishes a monitoring and evaluation advisory service.

2002

Focus on Results at Monterrey

The Monterrey Consensus underscores a shared responsibility for achieving development results. The multilateral development bank heads' statement outlines an approach to better managing for results.

First Results Roundtable

The multilateral development banks jointly sponsor an International Roundtable on Better Measuring, Monitoring, and Managing for Development Results, including representatives from client countries, development partners, and civil society.

Results Agenda

The Development Committee endorses the Bank's results agenda, reflecting commitments by developing and developed countries to a shared responsibility for achieving development results.

For staff learning and incentives, several Bankwide events, including Results: Everybody's Business (held in early January 2004), highlighted emerging good practices and sent strong signals throughout the institution on the importance of implementing the results agenda. More recently, the Open Exchanges Program featured cross-team learning on managing for results in country programs.

Fostering a global partnership on managing for development results
A formal partnership has been established through the Multilateral Development Bank Working Group and, more recently, through the Multilateral Development Bank/OECD–DAC Joint Venture on Managing for Development Results. For the global statistical community, more than a year of preparation resulted in agreement on a medium-term global action plan to strengthen international statistical systems. The Second International Roundtable on Managing for Development Results, in February 2004 in Marrakech, helped foster an emerging consensus on priorities for the global partnership.

More recently, the Paris High-Level Forum on Harmonization, Alignment, and Results provided an opportunity to strengthen the links between the harmonization and results agenda, and included the preparation of a list of expected results that countries and development partners will be using to strengthen mutual accountability for improving aid effectiveness. The Paris forum also provided a useful opportunity for sharing a draft of "Managing for Development Results: Principles in Action: Sourcebook on Emerging Good Practice," a first step toward building a community of practice among country practitioners concerned with building capacity in this area.

2003

Results Agenda Implementation Action Plan
The conceptual framework for Managing for Results is translated into a specific implementation action plan, discussed by the Committee on Development Effectiveness in December 2002 and finalized in January 2003.

Results-Based Country Assistance Strategy
The first pilot results-based country assistance strategy, for Sri Lanka, goes to the Board. The approach is adopted as standard practice two years later.

Focus on Results in Investment Lending
The revised Project Concept Note and Project Appraisal Document increase the focus on results in investment lending.

Multilateral Development Bank Working Group on Results
The multilateral development bank heads formally establish the MDB Working Group on Managing for Development Results during their meeting in Dubai.

MDB/OECD–DAC Joint Venture
The Joint Venture on Managing for Development Results is established within the DAC Working Party on Aid Effectiveness and Donor Practices.

Ongoing challenges

The concepts underlying the results agenda are based on common sense. But it is difficult to be effective if you have not defined your expected results or do not have systems for tracking progress toward their accomplishment—so there are many challenges to be faced in promoting management for results.

First, development outcomes at global, country, and local levels are influenced by many factors and stakeholders. Attributing change to an intervention of the Bank or other source of funds is often technically not possible. What is important is to find out what makes interventions effective, not whose dollar paid for the intervention.

Second, development agencies and their partners need to track trends in the performance of particular interventions and their outcomes, using reasonably accurate and reliable data, to identify where development problems are greatest and where investments are likely to have the highest payoff. Gaps in national and especially subnational information systems make this a difficult challenge. For example, most of the poorest countries do not have the underlying information infrastructure to ensure regular tracking of even basic demographic data except through ad hoc efforts, and decisionmakers understandably are more keen to allocate resources to solving development problems than to measuring them. While this tradeoff is understandable, the long-run costs can be significant.

Third, incentives matter. Whether at the country or at the agency level, managers and staff will not make the effort to measure and report on results, or use this information in decisionmaking, if there is no link between the information on results and the resources and conditions in which they are

2004

Results—Everybody's Business

Staff participate in the first Bankwide learning event focused on results.

Second Results Roundtable, Marrakech

The multilateral development bank heads and the chairman of the OECD's Development Assistance Committee endorse common principles on managing for development results.

STATCAP

The Board approves the Statistical Capacity Building Program aimed at improving countries' capacity to monitor core development outcomes.

Global Monitoring Report

The Bank and the IMF jointly release the first full *Global Monitoring Report*, reviewing progress on policies and actions of developing and developed countries and international institutions toward meeting the Millennium Development Goals and related outcomes.

Focus on Results in Development Policy Lending

A new operational policy and Bank procedures increase the focus on results in development policy lending.

working, or if nobody is asking for evidence of results. Asking staff to report on results when they have insufficient resources to complete the tasks they have been assigned is a recipe for disillusionment and disappointment. At the same time, focusing on performance and documentation of accomplishments can be highly motivating, even in resource-constrained settings.

Managing for results requires explicit recognition that it costs resources to collect, interpret and use information about performance, whether in the form of building robust statistical systems at the national level, or bearing the costs of improving internal management information systems at the agency level. The development policy world recognizes that failing to make the investment in learning and reporting about effectiveness puts at risk the entire development enterprise and the prospects for significant poverty reduction and growth.

Looking ahead

Today, the Bank is working on implementing the results agenda. Continuing leadership from all levels of staff and management is critical for this deepening to occur across all three pillars of the action plan.

Country capacity

Supporting countries in strengthening capacity to manage for results remains the most difficult longer-term challenge of the results agenda. In the near term, the Bank will be increasing advocacy and outreach on the importance of managing for results through regional workshops, and teams will intensify support within country assistance strategies to strengthen country capacity to manage for results.

2005

Reporting on Results in Operations

The new Implementation Status and Results report improves monitoring and reporting on results in operations.

Open Exchanges Program

A Bankwide learning event features cross-team learning on managing for results in country programs.

IDA14—Focus on Results

Building on the results framework inaugurated under IDA13, a Results Measurement System is adopted for IDA14 focusing on a set of 14 outcome indicators and IDA's contribution through the country assistance strategy.

Internal focus

Within the Bank, implementation will focus on expanding the coverage and improving the quality of results-based country assistance strategies and country assistance strategy completion reports, strengthening the monitoring and evaluation framework for sector strategies and global programs, developing a more comprehensive results reporting system, reinforcing technical support for task teams, and rolling out a revised staff learning program. Getting staff incentives right—particularly informal ones—remains a significant internal challenge in supporting countries to achieve sustainable development results.

Global partnership

The global partnership requires greater commitment and coordination of resources for strengthening country capacity, as well as increased donor willingness to harmonize reporting requirements. Building on work to identify and disseminate emerging practices on managing for the results, in 2005 the Multilateral Development Bank Working Group and OECD–DAC Joint Venture on Managing for Results will support country-led processes to use peer learning to benchmark and help build country capacity to manage for results.

During his presidency, Wolfensohn laid a good foundation for a results-oriented operational culture at the Bank. But it will take a few more years to see the fruits of these efforts. Just as monitoring delivery and quality took 10 or more years to mature and develop into useful systems, so the results agenda will take its time to mature and trickle through the organization and to our neediest clients. But we know this is the right direction, and we need to persist.

Harmonization and Results
The Paris High-Level Forum on Harmonization, Alignment, and Results strengthens the link between harmonization and results, resulting in a specific list of expected results for countries and development partners to use in strengthening mutual accountability for improving aid effectiveness.

Mainstreaming the Results-Based Country Assistance Strategy
A stocktaking of the results-based country assistance strategy proposes mainstreaming the approach.

Results Reporting
Consultations are under way on a proposed Bankwide Results Reporting System.

18

In his 1997 Annual Meetings address, Jim Wolfensohn stated, "My goal is to make the World Bank the first port of call when people need knowledge about development. By the year 2000, we will have in place a global communications system with computer links, videoconferencing, and interactive classrooms, affording our clients all around the world full access to our information bases—the end of geography as we at the Bank have known it."

Technology to support core business

The Bank had its operational strategy in place, but there was a need for a technology backbone to support the Bank's knowledge activities. In 1995 the Bank relied on e-mail as the main mode of communication and had a large number of data systems that did not communicate with each other. Audio-conferences were the exception. Online discussions or videoconferences were unheard of. And the Bank's country offices, then called resident missions, were constantly trying to catch up with what was going on in the rest of the world.

By 2005 the Bank had implemented a world-class, satellite-based communications infrastructure. It had also harmonized several hundred internal system applications down to a few. And it promoted the internal use of systems and applications so that teams could work together and collaborate even when operating from different locations in different time zones. World Bank–related information—data and reports—had become readily available for wide groups of interested parties through the Internet, interactive applications, and well-structured and searchable databases. The idea of "anytime, anywhere" may seem obvious now for a global institution that acts locally and works with many different constituencies, but to become reality it took inspired and energetic leadership.

1997

WorldLinks Launched

Uganda becomes the first country to participate in WorldLinks, a collaboration between the World Bank's World Links for Development Program and the nonprofit World Links Organization designed to help new generations learn about world cultures, encourage school-to-school project collaboration, and serve as an information channel for teachers around the world.

Network for Knowledge

In his Annual Meetings address, Wolfensohn states, "By the year 2000 we will have in place a global communications system with computer links, videoconferencing, and interactive classrooms, affording our clients all around the world full access to our information bases."

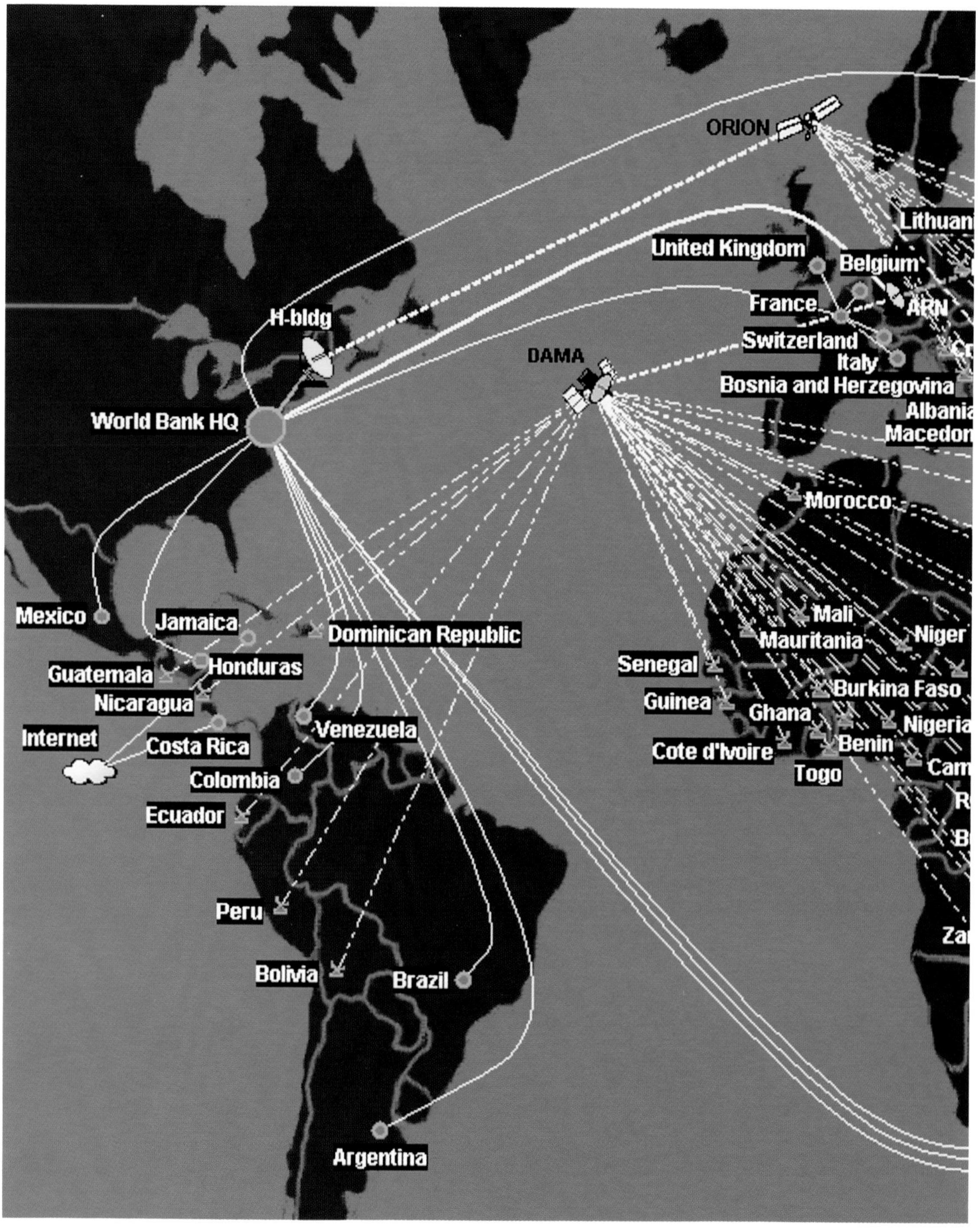
ORION
United Kingdom
Belgium
France
ARN
Switzerland
Italy
Bosnia and Herzegovina
H-bldg
DAMA
World Bank HQ
Morocco
Mexico
Jamaica
Dominican Republic
Guatemala
Honduras
Nicaragua
Internet
Costa Rica
Venezuela
Colombia
Ecuador
Peru
Bolivia
Brazil
Argentina
Mali
Mauritania
Niger
Senegal
Guinea
Ghana
Burkina Faso
Cote d'Ivoire
Benin
Togo

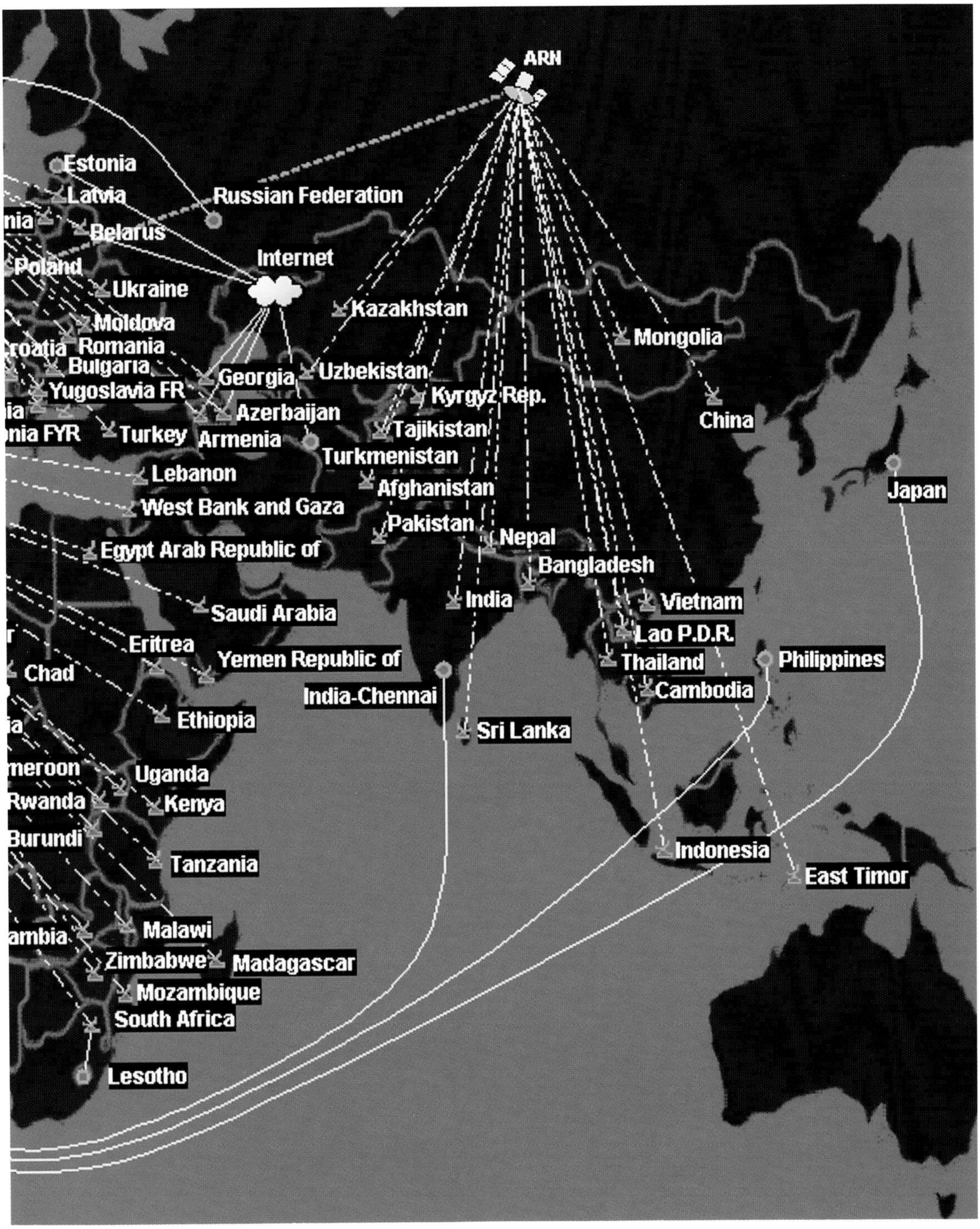
ARN
Estonia
Latvia
Russian Federation
Belarus
Poland
Internet
Ukraine
Kazakhstan
Moldova
Romania
Mongolia
Bulgaria
Georgia
Uzbekistan
Yugoslavia FR
Kyrgyz Rep.
Azerbaijan
China
Turkey
Armenia
Tajikistan
Turkmenistan
Lebanon
Afghanistan
Japan
West Bank and Gaza
Pakistan
Nepal
Egypt Arab Republic of
Bangladesh
India
Saudi Arabia
Vietnam
Lao P.D.R.
Eritrea
Chad
Yemen Republic of
Thailand
Philippines
India-Chennai
Cambodia
Ethiopia
Sri Lanka
Uganda
Rwanda
Kenya
Burundi
Tanzania
Indonesia
East Timor
Malawi
Zimbabwe
Madagascar
Mozambique
South Africa
Lesotho

Demonstrating that vision can translate to reality, Jim held up a card while delivering his speech at the World Bank's Annual Meetings in Dubai in 2003 and said, "We are making it possible for you to track information about your loans and your projects online, the same way that you can look up your credit card information online at any bank."

A time of rapid change

When Wolfensohn came to the Bank, the information technology (IT) landscape was quite different: no two computers were set up the same, and they were unreliable—some seemed to freeze almost daily. E-mail was used as a weak substitute for an actual network. Connectivity was slow and capacity was low. And only three country offices were connected to its headquarters network. The Bank had fragmented systems, mostly homegrown, and largely irreconcilable databases. Its information management and sharing was almost entirely paper-based. There were no electronic collaborative tools that would enable teams to work in a virtual space. Wolfensohn said, "Information technology is the central nervous system of the institution, which cannot function without a major transformation."

Becoming a more efficient Bank

The transformational journey needed bold direction from the top. Wolfensohn ordered that the highly stove-piped and fragmented IT organization structure be consolidated into the Information Solutions Group, with the mandate, "Make IT an integrating force, not a divisive one, and do it fast!"

In facing this transformational challenge, he asked that the Bank work on multiple tracks: integrate our business systems, build a global network, and

1999
A Global Network of Development Knowledge
The World Bank launches the Global Development Network with the primary objective of supporting the generation and sharing of knowledge for development. It officially becomes an independent body in 2001.

2000
First E-Bond
The World Bank's Treasury pioneers the world's first fully integrated global electronic bond offering over the Internet.

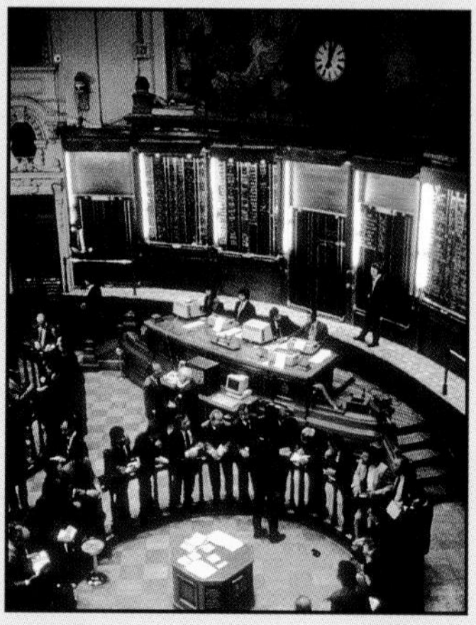

address the issue of fragmented business and knowlédge systems, so that decision-quality data, information, and knowledge could be shared internally and externally.

When he was told that there were 65-plus systems and 100-plus databases, he said, "Let's clean the kitchen and do it thoroughly." Although many thought that the mandate to integrate so many systems in such a short time was a nonstarter, in 18 months we "went live" globally with an integrated business system with information available in real time in 140 locations. Wolfensohn was there in the middle of the night when the switch was flipped.

Getting closer to the clients

To get the full benefits of the knowledge-sharing objectives and integrated systems, a global network was needed. Wolfensohn asked that this be put on a fast track. This had its own challenges: most of the countries have very poor infrastructure, and we had difficulty obtaining licenses. The program was so important to him that he would get on the phone and call heads of state and ministers of finance to request the granting of licenses.

What is in place now is a global electronic knowledge-sharing network, the most extensive high-speed videoconferencing network in the world (see map). Each day some 50 videoconferences connect 150–200 sites with distance learning and discussions on such issues as public sector reform, anticorruption, and HIV/AIDS. All our knowledge management, information, and business systems ride on the network, 24 hours a day, 7 days a week.

2001

WorldLinks Goes Global

More than 200 schools in 10 African countries participate in WorldLinks.

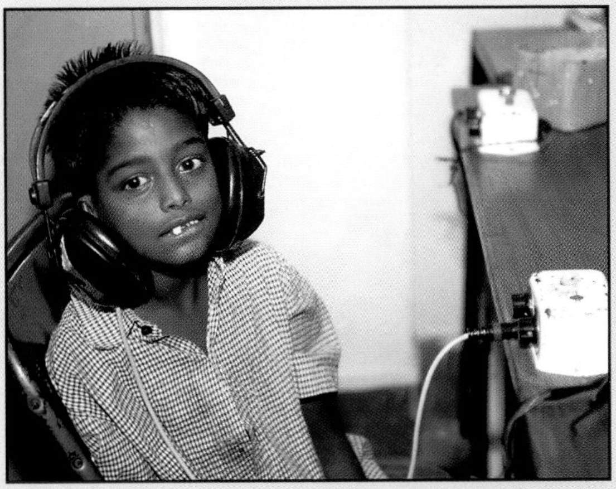

Development Gateway Launched

The Development Gateway builds partnerships and information systems to provide access to knowledge for development.

Putting clients first

But "cleaning the kitchen" wasn't enough. Wolfensohn also asked that better "food" be served to our clients. He wanted more support for client countries, through technology-enabled information projects that improve services to citizens and make governments more efficient and transparent through e-government programs.

On one of his early trips to Uganda he recognized that connectivity and knowledge sharing between children could be a powerful way to bridge the digital divide among youth. So he offered to use his own resources to connect three secondary schools with a high school in Jackson Hole, Wyoming. This was the genesis of WorldLinks, today a spun-off independent foundation that links students in developed and developing nations and builds capacity through professional development training for teachers. Since 1997 WorldLinks has reached more than 1.8 million students in more than 30 countries and trained more than 22,000 teachers.

As part of the Knowledge Bank initiative, Jim began to advocate that the Internet should be used more aggressively to address aid coordination—given the fragmentation in country programs—so that development knowledge and project information would be easily accessible on a neutral platform. The Development Gateway was incubated at the World Bank as a concept to address the issues, and as it gathered momentum, it was spun off to the Development Gateway Foundation. Today, it has more than 130,000 members, more than 300,000 monthly visitors, and an online network of more than 50 Country Gateways and 4 Research and Training Centers.

New Strategic Direction

The World Bank Institute embarks on a new strategic direction, becoming a capacity-development institute and expanding its capabilities to deliver demand-driven products and services at the country level.

Wolfensohn also supported other frontier-pushing initiatives, such as the e-bond, pioneered in 2000 by the Bank's Treasury. It was the world's first fully integrated global electronic bond offering over the Internet. The e-bond empowered all current and potential bond investors, whether small or large, to participate on the same financial conditions in a primary Bank bond offering. On another front, Jim was excited about providing online a wealth of data and analytical capability to clients, donors, and development practitioners through the Development Data Platform, launched by the Development Economics Group.

Using IT to its full effectiveness

"Wolfensohn viewed technology as the key to scale, not just for internal use but also for reaching outside the organization," noted a recent Harvard Business School case study—now part of the curriculum for MBA students—which considered the leadership aspect of the Bank's IT-enabled business transformation. Interviewing Wolfensohn for the study, Professor Warren McFarlan asked, "What keeps you awake at night about IT?" He answered, "I worry that we are not using IT to its full effectiveness."

"That," Wolfensohn said, "is our next challenge!"

Part Four

CHALLENGES AHEAD

THE GLOBAL DEVELOPMENT AGENDA WILL BE SHAPED BY POWERFUL FORCES IN the next decades: a more populous world, a world of greater wealth and greater inequality, demographic shifts toward more people in developing countries, greater urbanization, a realignment of geopolitical forces as some developing countries become important global economic players, a quest for global security in the face of terrorism, civil conflict, and failed states. Globalization and information technology will continue to create leapfrogging and business opportunities for some countries and increase risks for others.

The Bank will need to respond creatively to these challenges to spur sustained growth in developing countries and ensure a more equitable sharing of global wealth. There is reason to be optimistic and much to build on. The Bank's strategic framework—with its twin pillars of investing in and empowering people and promoting a favorable investment climate—provides a robust basis for scaling up its efforts. The centrality of the client in defining the country agenda has proved to be a solid foundation for sustainable development efforts. The greater presence of the Bank in countries through decentralization enhances its resilience and responsiveness. The Bank's extensive network of global partnerships and alliances provides a creative tension that greatly enhances its catalytic and leveraging role while ensuring that it remains dynamic and attuned to clients' needs. Maintaining a focus on results and continuing to place a premium on staff excellence and analytical rigor will sustain its credibility and enable it to continue its lead in influencing the development agenda.

But major challenges remain. To maintain its leadership in development, the Bank needs to embark on a four-part action agenda: scale up poverty reduction efforts, strengthen instruments for responding to a more differentiated clientele, mobilize more resources for development, and strengthen institutional effectiveness with a focus on results.

Scaling up efforts to reduce poverty

Poverty and inequality remain the central challenges of development. In the next 30 years the world will become wealthier, but the gap between the rich and the poor will widen. The absolute gap in per capita income between the world's poorest countries and the wealthiest will double by 2030. Scaling up action on poverty reduction will require action at the country and international level to anchor efforts to achieve the MDGs in country-led development, improve the environment for private-sector-led growth, expand human development services, dismantle barriers to trade, and increase the level and effectiveness of aid.

Responding to a spectrum of clients

There is a strong case for the Bank to remain engaged across the spectrum of developing countries, though the mix of services—knowledge, capacity development, and financing, including grants—will vary. The Bank is likely to continue providing nonfinancial services, even in client segments where the demand for finance is strong.

The recent task force on improving organizational effectiveness recommended that the Bank become more versatile and flexible to enable greater differentiation in business approaches across countries, to facilitate the simultaneous management of long-term predictable engagements and short-term opportunistic ones, and to deploy staff and resources across varying mixes of global and country programs. It has also recommended increasing synergies within the World Bank Group and developing a Bank Group strategy that will provide a more comprehensive package of products and services to meet the needs of the full range of clients.

Mobilizing more resources for development

International cooperation is likely to get stronger, not weaker. There is a consensus that aid is effective in combating poverty when it is provided to countries with good policies and is predictable, flexible and well coordinated. A strong push is needed to increase aid and to achieve the MDGs.

Increasing aid flows will require a comprehensive package of measures. In the short term it will be necessary to frontload aid through innovative global financing instruments. Several are under discussion: the International Finance Facility, global taxes, enhanced voluntary contributions, and blending arrangements. In the medium term rich countries will need to raise their official development assistance to the agreed target of 0.7 percent of gross national income, facilitate free and fair multilateral trading arrangements, and encourage private foreign direct investment. Under IDA14 it is expected that about 30 percent of the resources will be disbursed in the form of grants. In the medium term IDA will need to balance the benefits of the initiatives already under way—increasing the grant component of IDA lending and forgiving more of the debt of the heavily indebted poor countries—with IDA's long-term viability as a provider of concessional finance.

Efforts to increase aid will need to go hand in hand with greater aid effectiveness. The Bank has been a leading actor in the international efforts on aid harmonization. It needs to remain at the forefront in this, use its global experiences to help countries and partners scale up good practices, and develop transparent systems to monitor progress against commitments.

Fostering private capital flows

The volume of private capital flows to developing countries is much higher than that of official development assistance. This raises the issue of whether the Bank should withdraw from countries that have access to private capital. The experience of the last 10 years would indicate that it would be a strategic error to do so—for four reasons. First, more than 75 percent of net private capital flows are channeled to a dozen countries, among them some of the largest. This still leaves more than 100 developing counties with little access to private financing. Bank financing would fill this gap. Second, even in countries that have access to private capital, it does not generally finance basic infrastructure and social services. Third, middle-income countries are home to about 70 percent of the world's poor, and the Bank can help them target their pockets of poverty. Fourth, the Bank can productively harness the private sector to achieve development goals and ensure that poor people participate in and benefit from the growth process.

The struggle against hunger and poverty is the true path to reach global prosperity and, consequently, security and peace. Therefore, peace cannot be achieved without development, nor can development be achieved without social justice.

Luiz Inácio Lula da Silva
President of Brazil

Tackling global and cross-border issues

Globalization and the need for collective global action on an increasing number of cross-border issues have broadened the Bank's global partnership program. The Bank continues to be called on to play a direct and catalytic role in well-established programs such as trade, debt relief, and aid coordination and to scale up its engagement in newer ones including migration, money laundering, communicable diseases, and climate change. While the Bank is well positioned to provide leadership in these areas, an expanded global program is likely to create tension with the country focus, calling for a careful balance between the two.

Strengthening institutional effectiveness

At the end of the day, it is results on the ground that matter. The Bank has made significant progress in managing for results: results-based country assistance strategies and results frameworks for IDA programs and fostering global partnerships for the results agenda. The efforts are quite nascent and will need to be strengthened and scaled up.

Budget allocation processes have attempted to encourage selectivity as a means to ensure that the Bank does not become all things to all people. As this book demonstrates, the expansion in the Bank agenda has been in direct response to fundamental challenges facing its clients. While all the issues are therefore important, the Bank's catalytic role should not automatically translate into an implementation role. Instead, the Bank could work with partners to implement parts of its agenda. Examining tradeoffs and using resources flexibly will allow the Bank to respond to evolving needs. In particular, the budget allocation process needs to align incentives with the three core elements that give the Bank its competitive edge—results, staff excellence, and analytical rigor—and which are all highly susceptible to budget fluctuations. The decentralization process needs to be reviewed regularly against relative costs and the challenge of adjusting the size of country offices to volatile business volume.

As economic power spreads to countries in the South, their demand for greater voice and influence in the Bank will intensify. The ongoing work to increase "Voice" in the Board should provide a platform for realigning the Bank's governance structure with the nature and mix of its clients.

The world economy in 2050 is likely to be four times greater than it is today but the wealth will be inequitably distributed. There will be another 3 billion people posing enormous risks for the planet. An important role for the World Bank going forward must be to help poor countries manage these risks—with new technology, new infrastructure, new energy sources, new models of resources management, and new financial mechanisms for global public goods. These are all areas where the Bank and its development partners can ensure that actions taken today do not limit the range of development choices in 2050.

Postscript

JIM WOLFENSOHN'S CONTRIBUTION TO

THE DEVELOPMENT AGENDA

Views from the outside

FOUR LEADING DEVELOPMENT ECONOMISTS ADDED THEIR VIEWS ON JIM Wolfensohn's contribution to the development agenda.

Development as construction—by Amartya Sen

Jim Wolfensohn's ideas and commitment have been profoundly important not just for the World Bank, but for the world of economic development in general. He has played a major part in overcoming the severe view of development as a "fierce" process that constantly demands "blood, sweat, and tears." That stern view celebrates, reasonably enough, the need for some sacrifice in the interest of making things better in the future, but it tends also to focus to a surprising extent on surrender and immolation. The regimen that used to be commended—and sometimes firmly imposed—tended to be long on cutting what could be cut (including supportive institutional arrangements) and short on building what needed to be built (including the expansion, through societal support, of the practical ability of people to do what they want to do).

There is considerable similarity between Jim Wolfensohn's humane—and also more productive—conviction that what is needed is constructive help in advancing "comprehensive development" and Adam Smith's frustration that even those who understood his message about the importance of the market could not stretch beyond that to see that the market opportunities needed social initiatives to defend and supplement them. Jim's own critique is in tune with Smith's dismay that those in powerful economic and political positions often miss the creative role of social strengthening. Smith complained, for example, about the tendency of those in power to neglect the important fact that "for a very small expense the public can facilitate, can encourage, and can even impose upon almost the whole body of the people, the necessity of acquiring those most essential parts of education."

Neither Smith nor Wolfensohn saw blood and tears as big factors of production, even if some room could be found for healthy sweat. The last meeting at which I was privileged to speak under Jim's chairmanship was on the need to pay more attention to the predicament of the disabled. Jim's sympathetic understanding of the adversities of disability, which afflict, in one form or another, 600 million people (about 10 percent of the world population), fit in well with his general search for the ways and means of making disadvantaged people more productive and less handicapped. To understand the reach of Jim Wolfensohn's contributions, we have to recognize the constructive insights that Jim has brought to economic and social development.

It would, of course, be true to say that Wolfensohn has paid more attention to poverty than any of his predecessors, and that it is one of his major achievements to make poverty reduction the overarching priority of the World Bank. But that diagnosis, true enough as it is, is not an adequate measure of Jim's contribution. We also have to take fuller note of the power of his capacious understanding of the ways and means of removing poverty and deprivation. Given the reach of Wolfensohn's insights, his influence on the development community is not going to wane even as he moves on to other challenges away from the World Bank.

As Jim sorts out the interactive problems of Palestinians and Israelis (a tremendously important responsibility), he will have reason to take satisfaction also in the fact that the canals he has already built will continue to carry more and more water to more and more greens. We have reason to cheer for the future, not just celebrate the past.

Two pillars of development—by Sir Nicholas Stern

Success in fighting poverty and improving living standards and well-being in the developing world has three prerequisites. It requires, first, an understanding of the meaning of poverty and of development; second, an understanding of what drives them; and third, a strategy focused on these drivers, together with the ability to translate that strategy into action. Toward the beginning of his second term, in early 2001, Jim put to the Board a strategy, which it readily endorsed. That strategy, crystallizing the key ideas developed in his first term, came to be known in the Bank as "the two-pillar strategy."

The first pillar was founded on the recognition that overcoming poverty requires economic growth, and that growth is driven by the private sector. Importantly, in this strategy that sector was understood to range from the smallest and often most important type of private enterprise, the family farm, to the large modern firm. The conditions for growth, investment, and employment are shaped by governments, through what came to be called the "investment climate." This is shorthand for economic policy, infrastructure, and especially government behavior, including the degree of corruption and the effectiveness of institutions. Thus the first pillar in the strategy was the building of an investment climate conducive to private-sector growth and productivity. This is best achieved through an open, transparent, and constructive partnership with the private sector.

The second pillar—which is as important as the first and in fact reinforces it—was investing in and empowering people, particularly poor people. Empowerment would allow them to participate in growth, both as drivers and beneficiaries. This pillar, too, must be built and shaped by government, working in partnership with and accountable to the people and civil society. Empowerment should not be seen only as an instrument for achieving development—it is also a central element of development itself.

The two-pillar strategy, with its focus on institutions and government behavior and with its objective of overcoming poverty, goes far beyond the so-called Washington consensus, which focused largely on making sensible macroeconomic policy, improving the functioning of markets, and increasing trade. The strategy Jim promoted is much deeper and broader. It is about the institutions, behavior, and relationships that shape the lives of people. It is about overcoming poverty as poor people themselves define it. And it is about the promotion of an active state that serves its people.

The antithesis of this strategy is a state hobbled by pervasive corruption, one that preys on its people rather than serving them. Jim's insight and courage early in his first term led him to address corruption squarely through his speech at the World Bank–IMF Annual Meetings of 1996, and thereby set the Bank on a new course. This was a landmark in the Bank's approach to fighting poverty.

The principles, strategy, and sense of direction that Jim brought to the Bank, encapsulated in the two pillars, have reshaped the institution's approach to development. They have also advanced the understanding of development far beyond where it was in the mid-1990s when Jim arrived at the Bank. Ideas and insights that lead to strategies for effective action provide the most enduring of legacies.

The CDF's intellectual structure—by Joseph Stiglitz

Jim Wolfensohn's Comprehensive Development Framework (CDF) represented a major advance in development thinking and practice. Previously, development thinking and practice had been a quixotic quest for that single, quick fix that would ensure development success. At one time, that quick fix was money. It was thought that since developing countries had less capital than more developed countries, supplying more capital would do the trick. Indeed, that thinking provided part of the rationale for the World Bank: if a shortage of funds was the problem, clearly a bank was a key part of the solution.

Later, in the 1980s, there was a switch from projects to policies: the new watchword was structural adjustment, which involved trade liberalization, privatization, and macroeconomic stabilization. (Revealingly, "stabilization" typically meant stabilizing prices, not employment or output.) But these policies proved neither necessary nor sufficient for growth. We can see this in the experience of East Asian countries, which followed quite different policies but were more successful than other developing countries in terms of growth and poverty reduction. Education was another "single policy" solution that grabbed attention for a while but proved similarly incomplete as a tool for spurring development.

Early on at the Bank, Jim emphasized that developing countries were separated from developed countries by more than their lack of resources. There was also a gap in knowledge, which inspired Jim's emphasis on the need for a Knowledge Bank. He recognized that the world had moved into the Knowledge Economy, and that among the countries that had thrived in the new environment were India and the countries of East Asia—countries that had invested heavily not just in primary education but also in secondary and tertiary education, and especially in technology and science. This represented a major change in the Bank's approach to education, which previously had focused on primary education, and it was reflected in the *World Development Report 1998: Knowledge for Development.*

Jim's campaign against corruption also represented a major and much-needed advance in thinking about government, as the focus shifted from downsizing the state to improving the state. Failed and ineffective states were no less of an impediment to development than were overbearing states. The *World Development Report 1997* reflected this new attempt at finding the balanced role of the state, reflecting an understanding of the limitations both of markets and of the state.

These insights about development contributed to the CDF. The framework emphasized the need for each country to identify the facets of its economy—and of society more broadly—that were most in need of being strengthened. Identifying and acting on these key bottlenecks would yield returns elsewhere because of the strong linkages among the sectors. For example, improved productivity in the rural sector or better access to export markets would do little good if the country lacked roads and harbors for transporting crops. More positively, in a malaria-infested country, a malaria eradication program could increase production and even increase the effective land supply, as parts of the country that were almost uninhabitable because of infestation become livable. And if more individuals live longer because of better health, that would increase the returns to education and hence the incentive to invest in it.

The CDF also called for each developing country to participate more actively in identifying what needed to be done, as well as for greater collaboration among the donors in helping each country realize its objectives. As Jim put it, the CDF entailed "putting the country in the driver's seat," which marked a significant change in traditional relationships. It also enhanced the benefits from Jim's earlier initiative to decentralize the Bank's operations by moving country directors and staff into developing countries, bringing the Bank into closer contact with those living in the countries served by the Bank.

Some criticized the CDF as leading to a lack of focus. Those critics wanted a return to the good old days when the same prescriptions were applied to every country—and worked almost nowhere. On the contrary, the CDF was meant to sharpen the focus—but a focus that differed from one country to another, depending on country circumstances and objectives.

It is worth noting the contrast between the CDF and the shock-therapy approach that had failed so often. Shock therapy often seemed to emphasize comprehensiveness, in that it prescribed broad and rapid transformation of an economy on many fronts—though in practice the set of issues it focused on was relatively narrow. Shock therapy ignored the importance of the institutional infrastructure, which could neither be created overnight nor imposed from the outside. Indeed, even when not imposed from the outside, shock therapy too often entailed a top-down approach to reform. An essential aspect of the CDF, as conceived by Wolfensohn, was participation—a movement toward meaningful, participatory democracy that did not substitute for, but went well beyond, electoral democracy.

Jim has always emphasized the enormous scale of the task of eliminating poverty in the developing world. He has spoken repeatedly of the need to go beyond projects and policies—and of the importance of scaling up. The Comprehensive Development Framework provided an intellectual structure that was essential in accomplishing these ambitious goals. We have gone only a little way down the road that he helped lay out. There is much yet to be done.

Reducing global poverty—by Angus Deaton

Five or six years ago, around the middle of Jim Wolfensohn's time at the Bank, I attended a consultation in Delhi about the preparation of the *World Development Report 2000/2001: Attacking Poverty*. The World Bank manager who introduced the consultation explained to the audience that every 10 years the World Bank devoted the WDR to poverty to take stock of progress toward the Bank's ultimate mission.

When I heard the manager's claim, I was startled by its rewriting of history. It was true in the most literal sense: there had been major reports on poverty in 1980 and 1990, so that *Attacking Poverty* would indeed be the third in the sequence. But before Jim Wolfensohn's time, it was simply not true that the World Bank had consistently focused on a mission of poverty reduction. If there had been a *World Development Report* on poverty once a decade, it was only because the cycle of development fashion within the Bank took about 10 years to turn full circle. At that frequency, the Bank would come round to worrying about poverty, documenting it, and thinking about how to tailor policy to eliminate it. In between times, other views prevailed. There were (long) years when "getting prices right" was the keystone to economic growth and when there was no need to measure poverty, because there was no other possible policy. Dogma dominated data, making it largely superfluous.

Five years later, things are different. Under Jim Wolfensohn, the Bank's poverty reduction mission is clear, and it has held steady to that course for long enough so that even some of its sternest critics have begun to understand that the commitment to poverty reduction is for real, even if some will always disagree with the means. That, in itself, is an enormous change.

The institution has also become serious about monitoring poverty, which was never previously the case. The Millennium Development Goals mark to a significant degree the adoption of Wolfensohn's World Bank agenda by the world as a whole. And the lead goal, to reduce poverty by half by 2015, not only has the World Bank as a key player in its implementation, but also entrusts to it the score-keeping. The Bank is not only dedicated to a world free of poverty, it is now institutionally committed to keeping tabs on how it is doing.

Measurement and monitoring at the Bank have changed beyond all recognition. There used to be a great reluctance to collect data or to obtain secondary data, and even more reluctance to be its long-term repository. When Simon Kuznets looked at the relationship between growth, poverty, and inequality in 1955, he had data for six countries, three of which were rich. The Bank's first attempt to measure global poverty in 1979 had data (in many cases, very weak data) from 36 poor countries. In the latest version of the poverty counts, the Bank drew information from 454 surveys from 97 countries covering 93 percent of the population of all low- and middle-income countries. Wolfensohn's Bank has also taken over responsibility for the International Comparison Project, the giant global data collection effort that constructs the world's only measure for comparing living standards and poverty across countries. This data infrastructure, which is the basis for monitoring poverty around the world, gives substance to the "Knowledge Bank." It also signals the seriousness of the poverty reduction effort; without measurement, we might as well not bother, and the Bank will never persuade its critics, nor ought it to. This seriousness about reducing poverty is surely one of Jim Wolfensohn's finest legacies, not only to the Bank, but to the world.

CAS	country assistance strategy
CDF	Comprehensive Development Framework
CPIA	Country Policy and Institutional Assessment
CSOs	civil society organizations
EC	European Commission
GAVI	Global Alliance for Vaccines and Immunization
GDLN	Global Development Learning Network
HIPC	Heavily Indebted Poor Countries
HIV/AIDS	human immunodeficiency virus/acquired immune deficiency syndrome
IBRD	International Bank for Reconstruction and Development
IDA	International Development Association
IFC	International Finance Corporation
IMF	International Monetary Fund
LICUS	Low-Income Countries Under Stress
MDGs	Millennium Development Goals
MIGA	Multilateral Investment Guarantee Agency
NGO	nongovernmental organization
ODA	official development assistance
OECD/DAC	Organisation for Economic Co-operation and Development/Development Assistance Committee
OED	Operations Evaluation Department
PRGF	Poverty Reduction and Growth Facility
PRSP	Poverty Reduction Strategy Paper
RAAC	Risk-Adjusted Allocation of Capital
SDR	special drawing rights
TB	tuberculosis
UK	United Kingdom
UN	United Nations
UNAIDS	Joint United Nations Programme on HIV/AIDS
UNDP	United Nations Development Programme
UNICEF	United Nations Children's Fund
WBI	World Bank Institute
WDR	*World Development Report*
WHO	World Health Organization
WTO	World Trade Organization

Collier, P., V. L. Elliot, H. Hegre, A. Hoeffler, M. Reynal-Querol, and N. Sambanis. 2003. *Breaking the Conflict Trap: Civil War and Development Policy.* Washington D.C.: World Bank; New York: Oxford University Press.

Danaher, K., ed. 1994. *50 Years is Enough: The Case Against the World Bank and the International Monetary Fund.* Boston, Mass.: South End Press.

International Financial Institution Advisory Commission. 2000. *Report of the International Financial Institution Advisory Commission.* Washington, D.C.

Mallaby, S. 2004. *The World's Banker: A Story of Failed States, Financial Crises, and the Wealth and Poverty of Nations.* New York: Penguin Press.

McFarlan, F. W., and B. J. DeLacey. 2003. "Enabling Business Strategy with IT at the World Bank." Harvard Business School Publishing, Boston, Mass.

Narayan, D., with R. Patel, K. Schafft, A. Rademacher, and S. Koch-Schulte. *Voices of the Poor: Can Anyone Hear Us?* New York: Oxford University Press, published for the World Bank.

National Journal. 2005. "Global Conscience." January 29.

Ritzen, J. 2005. *A Chance for the World Bank.* London: Anthem Press.

Sen, A. *Development as Freedom.* New York: Oxford University Press.

UN Millennium Project. 2005. *Investing in Development: A Practical Plan to Achieve the Millennium Development Goals.* London: Earthscan.

Wolfensohn, J. 1999. "A Proposal for a Comprehensive Development Framework: A Discussion Draft." World Bank, Washington, D.C.

Wolfensohn, J., and F. Bourguignon. 2004. "Looking Back, Looking Ahead." Prepared for the 2004 Annual Meetings of the World Bank and the International Monetary Fund, October 3, Washington, D.C.

World Bank. 1995. *World Development Report 1995: Workers in an Integrating World.* New York: Oxford University Press.

———. 1996. *World Development Report 1996: From Plan to Market.* New York: Oxford University Press.

———. 1997. *World Development Report 1997: The State in a Changing World.* New York: Oxford University Press.

———. 1999. *World Development Report 1998/1999: Knowledge for Development.* New York: Oxford University Press.

———. 2000. *World Development Report 1999/2000: Entering the 21st Century: The Changing Development Landscape.* New York: Oxford University Press.

———. 2001a. *Engendering Development: Through Gender Equality in Rights, Resources, and Voice.* New York: Oxford University Press

———. 2001b. *World Development Report 2000/2001: Attacking Poverty.* New York: Oxford University Press.

———. 2002. *World Development Report 2002: Building Institutions for Markets.* New York: Oxford University Press.

———. 2003a. "A New Global Balance: The Man, His Message, His Music." Video prepared for the 70th birthday and related transcripts on CD-ROM.

———. 2003b. *World Development Report 2003: Sustainable Development in a Dynamic World: Transforming Institutions, Growth, and Quality of Life.* New York: Oxford University Press.

———. 2004a. *Focus on Sustainability 2004.* Washington, D.C.

———. 2004b. "Supporting Development Programs Effectively: Applying the Comprehensive Development Framework Principles: A Staff Guide." Washington, D.C.

———. 2004c. *World Development Report 2004: Making Services Work for Poor People.* New York: Oxford University Press.

———. 2005a. *Economic Growth in the 1990s: Learning from a Decade of Reform.* Washington, D.C.

———. 2005b. *Global Monitoring Report 2005: Millennium Development Goals: From Consensus to Momentum.* Washington, D.C.

———. 2005c. "Improving Women's Lives: World Bank Actions since Beijing." Gender and Development Group, Washington, D.C.

———. 2005d. *World Development Report 2005: A Better Investment Climate for Everyone.* New York: Oxford University Press.

Cover
Top left: Robert L. Floyd
Top center: Arne Hoel/World Bank
Top right: Tran Thi Hoa/World Bank Photo Collection
Bottom: Eric Miller/World Bank Photo Collection

Back Cover
World Bank

Title Page
World Bank Photo Collection

Overview
Opener: Tran Thi Hoa/World Bank Photo Collection
p. 2 IMF
p. 3 World Bank
p. 4 Steven Harris/World Bank Photo Collection
p. 6 (left) Deborah Campos/World Bank; (right) Alfredo Srur/World Bank Photo Collection
p. 7 Deborah Campos/World Bank
p. 8 Deborah Campos/World Bank

Part One
Opener: Michael Foley
p. 10 Lianqin Wang
p. 13 Arne Hoel/World Bank
p. 14 Michael Foley
p. 15 Michael Foley
p. 16 Deborah Campos/World Bank
p. 17 Tran Thi Hoa/World Bank Photo Collection
p. 18 Michael Foley
p. 19 Michael Foley
p. 20 Curt Carnemark/World Bank Photo Collection
p. 23 Alejandro Lipszyc/World Bank Photo Collection
p. 24 Arne Hoel/World Bank
p. 25 Masaru Goto/World Bank Photo Collection
p. 26 Robert L. Floyd
p. 27 Trevor Samson/World Bank Photo Collection
p. 28 (left) Abigail Tamakloe/IFC; (right) Greg Girard/IFC
p. 29 (left) Sid Edelmann/IFC; (right) John Fiege/IFC
p. 31 John Fiege/IFC
p. 36 Arne Hoel/World Bank
p. 38 Arne Hoel/World Bank
p. 39 Michael Foley
p. 40 (left) Edwin Huffman/World Bank Photo Collection; (right) Tran Thi Hoa/World Bank Photo Collection
p. 42 Courtesy of Exxon-Mobil
p. 44 Curt Carnemark/World Bank Photo Collection
p. 45 Tim Cullen/World Bank Photo Collection
p. 46 Curt Carnemark/World Bank Photo Collection
p. 47 John Kagia
p. 48 World Bank
p. 49 Masaru Goto/World Bank Photo Collection
p. 50 Curt Carnemark/World Bank Photo Collection
p. 51 Masaru Goto/World Bank Photo Collection
p. 53 (left) Curt Carnemark/World Bank Photo Collection; (right) Masaru Goto/World Bank Photo Collection
p. 54 World Bank
p. 56 World Bank
p. 57 Michael Foley
p. 58 World Bank Photo Collection
p. 61 Bill Lyons/World Bank Photo Collection
p. 62 Jeremy Woodhouse/Getty Images
p. 63 Arne Hoel/World Bank
p. 64 Trevor Samson/World Bank Photo Collection
p. 65 Michael Foley
p. 66 Francis Dobbs/World Bank Photo Collection
p. 67 Michael Foley
p. 70 Curt Carnemark/World Bank Photo Collection
p. 72 Michael Foley

Part Two
Opener: Alfredo Srur/World Bank Photo Collection
p. 77 World Bank Photo Collection
p. 78 Arne Hoel/World Bank
p. 79 Alan Gignoux/World Bank Photo Collection
p. 80 Robert L. Floyd
p. 81 Arne Hoel/World Bank
p. 82 Tran Thi Hoa/World Bank Photo Collection
p. 84 Michael Foley
p. 85 Bill Lyons/World Bank Photo Collection
p. 87 James W. Adams
p. 88 Michael Foley
p. 89 Bill Lyons/World Bank Photo Collection
p. 90 Arne Hoel/World Bank
p. 92 Arne Hoel/World Bank
p. 93 Arne Hoel/World Bank

Part Three
Opener: Curt Carnemark/World Bank Photo Collection
p. 99 Arne Hoel/World Bank
p. 100 Michael Foley
p. 101 Michael Foley
p. 102 Arne Hoel/World Bank
p. 103 Trevor Samson/World Bank Photo Collection
p. 104 Deborah Campos/World Bank
p. 105 Arne Hoel/World Bank
p. 106 Dominic Sansoni/World Bank Photo Collection
p. 107 Arne Hoel/World Bank
p. 108 Ann Maest/IFC
p. 109 Michael Foley
p. 110 (left) Alfredo Srur/World Bank Photo Collection; (right) Anatoliy Rakhimbayev/World Bank Photo Collection
p. 111 Alfredo Srur/World Bank Photo Collection
p. 112 Michael Foley
p. 113 Alfredo Srur/World Bank Photo Collection
p. 114 Ami Vitale/World Bank Photo Collection
p. 116 Maria C. Velez/World Bank Photo Collection
p. 117 Alan Gignoux/World Bank Photo Collection
p. 118 Padraic Hughes/IMF
p. 120 World Bank
p. 121 World Bank
p. 122 World Bank
p. 123 World Bank
p. 124 (left) Anvar Ilyasov/World Bank Photo Collection; (right) Tran Thi Hoa/World Bank Photo Collection
p. 125 (left) World Bank; (right) Dominic Sansoni/World Bank Photo Collection
p. 126 Shehzad Noorani/World Bank Photo Collection
p. 127 Ami Vitale/World Bank Photo Collection
p. 128 Eric Miller/World Bank Photo Collection
p. 130 Alejandro Lipszyc/World Bank Photo Collection
p. 133 Alan Gignoux/World Bank Photo Collection
p. 134 Arne Hoel/World Bank
p. 135 Eric Miller/World Bank Photo Collection
p. 138 Curt Carnemark/World Bank Photo Collection
p. 139 (left) John Isaac/World Bank Photo Collection; (right) Masaru Goto/World Bank Photo Collection
p. 140 Thomas Sennett/World Bank Photo Collection
p. 141 Alan Gignoux/World Bank Photo Collection

Part Four
Opener: Ami Vitale/World Bank Photo Collection

Postscript
Opener: Michele Iannacci/World Bank